Dear Uncle Stanley

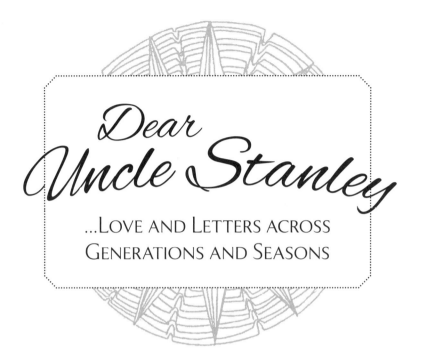

Dear Uncle Stanley
...Love and Letters across Generations and Seasons

By Ellen Doyle, OSU
Grand-niece of Monsignor J. Stanley Hale (1899–1985),
Beloved pastor of St. Mary's Church, Worthington, Minnesota,
and uncle to more than he ever knew.

Orange *frazer* Press
Wilmington, Ohio

ISBN 978-1949248-777
Copyright ©2023 Ellen Doyle, OSU
All Rights Reserved

No part of this publication may be reproduced in any material form (including photocopying or storing in any medium by electronic means and whether or not transiently or incidentally to some other use of this publication) without the written permission of the copyright holder except in accordance with the provisions of Title 17 of the United States Code.

Published for the copyright holder by:
Orange Frazer Press
37½ West Main St.
P.O. Box 214
Wilmington, OH 45177

For price and shipping information, call: 937.382.3196
Or visit: www.orangefrazer.com

Front cover image: Uncle Stanley, Wrightsville Beach,
North Carolina, late 1970s.

Back flap cover image: Ellen and Uncle Stanley, Ursuline Academy,
Cincinnati, Ohio, late 1970s

Names have been changed in some cases for privacy.

Book and cover design:
Orange Frazer Press with Catie South

Library of Congress Control Number: 2023910747

First Printing

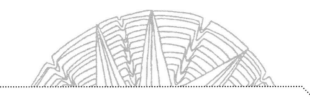

For Ellen (Nell) Isabelle Quinn Hale
July 25, 1897–September 27, 1978
My beloved grandmother and first correspondent.

Tributes

From Mary Pierce Brosmer, Founder,
Women Writing for (a) Change:

"Ellen Doyle, OSU creates with and for us the very experience her memoir chronicles: a loving correspondence across generations, a treasure trove of enduring wisdom and reciprocity: "the extraordinary gift of being taken seriously."

The reader, addressed as 'Dear One,' is taken seriously enough to receive Ellen's letters, as well as those of her Uncle Stanley, a life-loving, compassionate, erudite priest born in 1899. Both J. Stanley Hale and Ellen provide profound companionship and spiritual direction: 'While we had occasional face-to-face visits and phone calls, it was in our letters that we revealed the heart within our souls to each other. Written words seemed to contain our beings and our love like a precious earthen-ware jar, while spoken words seeped away as through a sieve.'

As someone who has spent decades practicing and teaching others writing as a way of listening to our inner lives and to those of others, I have seldom read a book which makes a more poignant case for the intimacy and power of the written word than *Dear Uncle Stanley*."

From Grace Manion, Undergraduate student at Villanova University,
eldest daughter of three, and avid fan of writing words of affirmation:

"In this beautiful exchange of letters, Sister Ellen Doyle invites readers, young and old, into a new relationship. Her words to the reader feel like the loving words of God the Father or like a hug from your grandmother when you were a little kid. Uncle Stanley's wisdom, guidance, and love shows just how much we have to learn from one another—no matter the differences between us. With a humble heart, I take these words and know I still have so much life to live. And so I will lean on others, let them guide me, and take every moment as it comes because it might just change my life."

....

From Father Jerry Mahon, Rector/Pastor of the Co-Cathedral of St. John the Evangelist, Rochester, Minnesota:

"While I was a young priest serving what was, in the early seventies, called the Diocese of Winona, Southern Minnesota, I visited St. Mary's Parish in Worthington, Minnesota. I was the Vocations Director for the diocese and so spent a fair amount of time traveling. On this particular visit, I came face to face with my mother's former Religion Teacher, Msgr. J. Stanley Hale. She had been a student of his in 1928 at what was then St. John's Catholic High School in Rochester, Minnesota. As a child, I remember my mother speaking of him often to us kids and she always said she would never forget his face. Ninety-five years after her high school experience and many years after listening to her recollections, I am the Rector/Pastor of the Co-Cathedral of St. John the Evangelist, the same Church/School where Msgr. Hale taught my mother.

Who is this exceptional human being who was ordained a priest and who encouraged all of us 'to live always the real intensity?' Honestly, J. Stanley witnessed to the truth of Christ as a real presence by recognizing and affirming the humanity of the people he served. Ellen Doyle, OSU, shares this truth through letters from her beloved grand-uncle, J. Stanley and you are in for an adventure of discovering the exceptional presence of Christ in the humanity of a passionate follower of the Mystery of Love.

This beloved pastor loved people and stayed with them through great joy and deep sorrow. He recognized their need and believed that Christ was the presence they longed for in everyday life. As a brilliant academician, he never got lost in an ideology, but looked for an authentic encounter with the people he discipled. *Dear Uncle Stanley*'s personal letters and the depth of the relationship revealed opens this path for all of us!!"

....

From Tim Flanagan, Founder, Catholic Leadership Institute:

"As an eighty-year-old grandfather in the winter season of my life, I discovered in Sr Ellen's and Monsignor Hale's letters great joy about my life journey. They even motivated me to dig out the letters my wife and I exchanged when I was in the Army! And helped me recognize more clearly the hope I have for our Church and world from my 30 years mentoring and learning with two generations of young seekers at the Catholic Leadership Institute. I encourage anyone seeking hope in your own intergenerational connections to read and share *Dear Uncle Stanley*."

Table Of Contents

The Letters In Four Seasons

Preface — xiii

In the Season of Spring

- THE WAY OF WRITING — 3
  - ON THE BEGINNING OF OUR WRITING
    - LETTERS TO ONE ANOTHER *(Letter 1)* — 3
  - ON GETTING MAIL *(Letter 4 and Excerpt from* Worthington Globe*)* — 10
  - ON WRITING MACHINES AND CYBERSPACE *(Letter 86)* — 15
  - ON THE GHOSTS OF CHRISTMAS *(Letter 62)* — 20
  - ON ORDINARY TIME *(Letter 18)* — 24

- SEEKING ANOTHER WAY — 29
  - ON TRAVEL *(Letter 2)* — 29
  - ON SECRETS *(Letter 10)* — 34
  - ON INNER ROOMS AND OTHER SACRED PLACES *(Letter 50)* — 38
  - WHERE SILENCE REIGNS AND SOLACE LIES *(Letter 69)* — 43
  - ON STAYING HOME *(Letter 110)* — 46
  - ON PRAYER AND HOLINESS *(Letters 6, 100, Article from* The (Winona Diocesan) Courier, *and Excerpt from* Uncle Stanley homily at Final Vows*)* — 49

In the Season of Summer

- LOVING & BEFRIENDING — 63
  - ON FAST FRIENDS AND LONG LOVES *(Letters 55, 156)* — 63
  - ON PEN PALS AND SOULMATES *(Letters 41, 100, 194, 153)* — 70
  - ON MANY MARYS *(Letters 28, 76, 131)* — 81
  - ON NEIGHBORS: HAVING THEM, BEING ONE, LIVING NEAR THEM, LOVING THEM *(Letters 11, 32, 80, 149)* — 93
  - ON CECILIA *(Letters 142, 155 and* Uncle Stanley's last letter to Cecilia*)* — 106

- TEACHING & MENTORING — 113
  - ON CHEMISTRY TESTS AND RETORTS *(Letters 60, 71)* — 113

ON TIGHTROPE-WALKING AND OTHER BALANCING TRICKS (Letter 19)	119
ON YES AND NO AND I DON'T KNOW (Letters 90, 104, 150)	122
ON WOMEN (Letter 112)	130
ON ZOOMING ACROSS TIME ZONES (Letter 167)	134

In the Season of Autumn

DELECTABLE DELIGHTS	139
ON GLEE (Letters 63, 74, 91)	139
ON CULINARY AND POETIC ARTS (Letters 96, 164)	145
ON BIRDS AND BEASTS (Letter 118)	152
ON GREAT BOOKS (Letter 132)	155
ON QUIZZICAL LOOKS AND OTHER GLANCES (Letter 178)	159
MAPS AND OTHER PATHWAYS	163
ON PRIDE AND PLENITUDE (Letter 79, Letter from Bishop Watters in response to Uncle Stanley's request to retire)	163
ON GETTING LOST (Letter 38)	170
ON LIFE DISCERNMENT AND DECISION-MAKING (Letters 26, 184)	175
ON RETIREMENT (Letters 172, 54, and Excerpt from Farewell Sermon to St Mary Parish)	181
ON AGING (Letter 3)	186

In the Season of Winter

KEEPING VIGIL	193
ON FAMILY TREES, BRANCHES AND ROOTS (Letters 39, 144)	193
ON EVERLASTING REBELLION AND OVERREACHING LOVE (Letter 43)	199
ON JUBILEE (Letter 84)	203
ON WILLS, BEQUESTS AND OTHER TREASURES (Letter 125)	207
ON WAITING (Letter 152)	212
ON WINTER (Letters 7, 29, 193)	216
ON LAST THINGS	225
THE LAST THREE LETTERS (Letters 198, 199, 200)	225

Epilogue	231
Acknowledgments	235

Preface

I was just eighteen when I received my first letter from Uncle Stanley, Great-Uncle Stanley. The extraordinary gift was that he took me seriously, responding quickly to the letter I wrote him from Nags Head, North Carolina, where I was on vacation with my family that last summer before I left home. Thus began a correspondence that would last eighteen years and seventy-two seasons, ending with his death at age eighty-six just as summer was about to turn toward autumn.

A large-spirited tall man with a thick crop of white hair, a ruddy face and a boisterous Irish laugh, Uncle Stanley drew young and old alike into his warm hugs and engaging conversation. But it was through the written word, mostly letters, that he established and deepened relationships that would enrich the lives of dozens of correspondents as well as his own. Educated in Europe, this priest-son of Irish immigrants was as intensely interested in the world, its religions, politics, art and literature, as he was in the developing faith, relationships, professional life and vocation of this grand-niece of his.

Fifty years younger than he, I intuitively knew that my eternal questions, youthful idealism, joys and sorrows would be safe in his keeping. What I couldn't have known was that our relationship would develop into one where his own tentative thoughts and feelings around aging, retirement, and death were safe with me. Nor that in the several decades since his death I would discover how deeply his love and wisdom has infused my life with meaning and joy.

Not long before he died, Uncle Stanley shared the Hale Family Tree he had complied with his ancestors and descendants. Extending from the branch Uncle Stanley shared with my grandfather, Desmond Hale, I am just a twig. Uncle Stanley had twenty-three nieces and nephews in my mother's generation and sixty-five grands in my generation. I nevertheless

"Fly it," envelope, March 1970.

knew before I was twenty that I was a favorite, one of "the nieces," as he called a few of us.

A typical "Uncle Stanley letter," as they came to be called by my friends, was three typed, single-spaced pages of plain white paper. The early ones, written in the days of optional domestic airmail at a higher rate, included the words "Fly it!" on the corner of the envelope, as if his bold black exuberant handwriting could add urgency to the airmail stamp and put his letter in my hands sooner. (In those days, snail mail, at the standard postal rate, traveled in a truck. Airmail, at a higher rate, traveled by plane and arrived sooner!) That first letter arrived three weeks before I left home to enter the Ursulines of Brown County Convent in St. Martin, Ohio, where I would spend my novitiate in training to become a nun. Over the years and seasons of our correspondence, I would receive two-hundred of these letters. Each one contained musings on his own busy life, stories of people he cared about, rants against inclement weather, enthusiasm for the changing church and nation, reflections on his extensive reading, and always a wise and loving response to my own sharing.

While we had occasional face-to-face visits and phone calls, it was in our letters that we revealed the heart within our souls to each other. Written words seemed to contain our beings and our love like a precious earthenware jar, while spoken words seeped away as through a sieve. We each crossed two generations in our letters to each other. He connected me to early family roots, to cultural and spiritual mentors, and to the experience of an aging man. I connected him to the dreams and idealism of youth, to a new generation of ministers in the church, and to the experience of a young adult woman.

Recognizing their universal wisdom and appeal, I shared many letters from this Uncle-soul-mate of mine with those whom I was coming to love and trust, several of whom became correspondents with him on their own. Themes of finding one's vocation and mentoring the next generation are interwoven with aging and approaching death. Stories of trying out new recipes are told beside those about family roots. Each season appears in poetic imagery. Contemplation and love of God are lifted up as delights for both old age and the young. Ordinary days filled with ordinary encounters with ordinary people are enriched by the extraordinary love and trust between us.

Before our letters to one another, Uncle Stanley and I would only meet in large family gatherings during summer trips from Cincinnati to Minnesota where the first five children in our family were born and where all our extended family still lived. On our first trip back west, I was just seven and already a novice letter-writer! I had just finished second grade with Sr. Mary, one of the Ursulines at St. Vivien, my Cincinnati grade school. What impressed me about the Ursulines and eventually drew me to join them was each one's unique personality with no two alike and each one discerning her own path in the midst of a community of faith. Uncle Stanley was not part of my discernment to enter the community, though he cheered me on without reserve once he knew of my decision, made during the fall of my senior year of high school.

Much later, in my early-forties and at about the midpoint of my eleven-year tenure as President of Chatfield College, I was wrestling with whether the time had come to move on from the college. Tired and discouraged, I wondered if I had given all I had to give. It was Ash Wednesday evening and for the first time in my life, I chose to skip church services so I could draw on Uncle Stanley's wisdom. He had been dead about ten years. For the first time in my life, I re-read a portion of his letters, the ones closest to his death. Although he died three months before I accepted the call to leadership at Chatfield, Uncle Stanley lifted up for me in the words of his last thirty-five letters just what I needed to face the challenges before me with confidence and courage.

I experienced those letters as a two-way mirror, reflecting back to me the values, instincts and ideals that still guide me in my life and put me in touch with this dear Uncle, now on the other side of a new life. Through the eyes of someone whose stance toward life was exuberant, whose wisdom was grounded in centuries of faith and culture, and whose love for me was unconditional, I saw my inner being so clearly that spring evening in Uncle Stanley's words to me that I effortlessly made the decision to recommit to serve as Chatfield's president for several more years. Uncle Stanley was there guiding me, cheering me on, loving me beyond his written words, given to me so many years before. Uncle Stanley's honesty about my gifts and limitations, his deep affection and good humor and his abiding faith in God were still reliable resources for me and others as we pursued new questions at a new stage of life.

Our words to one another alternated in another age but I do not have my letters to him. I discovered in his letter #125 that he had saved all of my letters just as I had saved his to me. Uncle Stanley spoke in that letter of dismantling his library and giving personal things away. He offered to mail my letters back to me. There were probably well over 100 of them at that point, given that we typically exchanged letters about once a month. I did not ask for them. He went on to live another six years, remaining in active communication with me until just a few days before he died.

Even without my own letters though, as I re-read Uncle Stanley's letters again at this winter season of my life, I am full of gratitude. Now at the age Uncle Stanley was when he answered my first letter to him, I am inviting

PREFACE

you to witness how an aging priest and his young niece companioned one another into life. My own letters written to you emerge from his letters to me long ago. And from my hope that our letters motivate you to reach out to a niece, an uncle, a grandchild, a mentor to share your own pondering about life across one or two generations and your own seasons.

As private as love letters and (almost!) as public as his weekly London Tablet, his treasured words and our loving relationship now seem meant for others. Even so, I timidly hold these words close to my own heart, knowing they reveal my soul and that of the great-uncle who loved me.

Dear Uncle Stanley

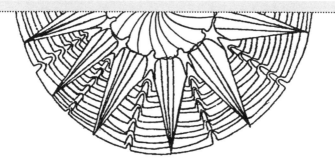

The Letters in Four Seasons
In the Season of Spring

As I now recognize, the season of childhood for those of us who are well-loved, is magical. With its tenuous secrets and tiny victories, it sprouts like spring in ways that are both delicate and fearless. In my case, my parents gave me a firm foundation made up of both the watered soil of unconditional love and the seedlings of responsibility that gave me the confidence and life experience that has served me my entire life. The little I know of Uncle Stanley's childhood is that it was his mother who taught him to be a letter-writer as a boy. Also that as a middle child with seven siblings, he empathized with his older brother, my grandfather Desmond James Hale. As the family's first-born son, Grandpa Hale carried the responsibility for the family business his whole life. Perhaps his intuitive understanding of Grandpa was what made Uncle Stanley so supportive of me. Although I was thrust into adulthood prematurely at age fourteen, I give thanks for my privileged vantage point from which to delight in the springtime childhoods of my seven younger siblings and now, their children and grandchildren. And for the little hints of my own springtime season that break ground in my memory from time to time.

The Way of Writing

On the Beginning of Our Writing Letters to One Another

> "I love the dark hours of my being.
> My mind deepens into them.
> There I can find, as in old letters,
> the days of my life, already lived,
> and held like a legend, and understood.
> Then the knowing comes: I can open
> to another life that's wide and timeless…."
> —From "The Dark Hours of My Being,"
> *Rilke's Book of Hours* by Rainer Maria Rilke

> "Among the minor blessings in life there is nothing
> so satisfying as a big, fat letter."
> —Uncle Stanley, letter 1

Dear One,

Perhaps you are wondering how these letters (from me to Uncle Stanley, him to me, me to you) came to be…and how they now come to be in your hands…

As I hinted earlier, it was in July 1967, during our family vacation to North Carolina's Outer Banks, when I wrote Uncle Stanley that first letter. I had seen him briefly in Minnesota a few weeks earlier when I traveled to visit my grandmother, her high school graduation gift for me.

I know from his response that in that first letter of mine that I caught him up on the story of my National Science Foundation Program at Ohio State University the summer before. I had been sorting out philosophies of

Ellen, Uncle Stanley, and Grandma Hale in St. Martin, Ohio, for final vows in 1973.

life with the brightest, agnostic, Jewish, and male minds of my generation. While reading James Thurber at 2:00 AM, playing soccer on Saturday mornings and solving theoretical math problems without a single integer for ten hours a day over ten weeks, I was discerning my life's path.

It was during that summer, in between my junior and senior years of high school, that I set my intention to join the Ursulines of Brown County, an idea that had been germinating since seventh grade. In May of my freshman year of high school, our youngest sibling was born and my mother remained in the hospital for an extended time with serious complications. Just fourteen years-old, I soloed in the mother-role for seven siblings, including Amy, our newborn and had the house we were selling ready for real estate agents to show it off. When Dad woke me in the night to tell me Mom was not expected to live and if I could handle things, I proudly assured him that I could. Thank God, Mom lived through that crisis. But for me, I grew up that May and was clear about what I felt was my call, and what wasn't. It would be well into the fall of senior year though before I would give voice to that decision in the midst of my mother's grief over her closest friend's terminal cancer.

My own sadness was that what felt like a holy and exciting call was an additional source of grief for Mom. Mom had married while a sophomore in college, giving up dreams to become a surgeon for Dad and what would become a family of eight children. I think she wanted me to follow that path too, or at least not to make a life-decision at an age too young to know any better. But with sixteen years of experience mothering my siblings, I felt I knew what I was saying no to. My mother reached out to Uncle Stanley to ask him to come to Cincinnati that next spring to talk me out of such a crazy idea. I remember his visit, but not any efforts to talk me out of my plans to enter the Ursuline community in September 1967.

Uncle Stanley, Ellen and Grandma Hale, in Madelia, Minnesota, 1960.

Also in my first letter to Uncle Stanley, I included a description of the oil painting of our Nags Head beach rental cottage that I created from a lawn chair in the sand that summer. A few colored towels hanging in the breeze at the side of the cottage proved that it was occupied, but, in my mind's eye to this day, I think of that cottage as empty. Of course, it would have been empty at the time I was painting it (at mid-morning when my seven siblings and my parents would have been playing in the surf or at its turbulent edge, some hundred yards over my right shoulder). My painting time was a way to practice what I had learned in art classes of course, but more importantly, it was a time of solitude, a time to contemplate the life I was about to begin without distraction.

For some reason, it also seemed noteworthy to tell him about one of our beach adventures, an activity that gave two or three of us pleasure one afternoon as we set out for an ice-cream cone or some errand. We decided to stand in the "hitchhikers' pose," facing traffic and walking backwards, but waving instead of actually trying to hitch a ride. We counted how many people responded with a wave. And boo-ed at those who ignored us. It seemed like a friendly thing to do in the midst of the Vietnam War and the Civil Rights movement. My siblings and I did our best to out-do one another in our efforts to get a response and found the occasional wave from strangers to be a huge victory.

I sent that first letter off in time for him to write me back just before I left home. He signed his first letter to me: Fr. S. I must have answered it quickly and addressed it Dear Uncle Stanley because, beginning with letter #2, he always signed his letters Uncle Stanley.

But Uncle Stanley was not my first correspondent. I actually became a letter writer when I was barely seven. I reached out on my own to write to my dear grandmother, Ellen Isabelle Quinn Hale, who went by Nell. I was named after her. We had left her behind in Madelia, Minnesota, when our family moved to Cincinnati. With child-like confidence I trusted that she would welcome hearing from me. And writing to her somewhat assuaged the grief of no longer living just three blocks away from her and Grandpa. Like our visits at her house, my letters became a private place for giving voice to what was on my young mind and heart. I would put the words on paper, read them over once, fold the paper twice, insert it in an envelope, address the envelope, lick and adhere the stamp and send it off. And then wait. A loving response always came.

These many decades later, I am still a letter-writer! My letters to YOU, dear One, may spring from a prompt from one of Uncle Stanley's letters. Or maybe I will find resources and ideas in my journals, my memories, a poem or just my point of view now, more than fifty years after I took a risk to reveal my soul to an uncle who lived nearly a thousand miles away.

Most importantly, I invite YOU to find and share your OWN voice, your own words, stories, mind and heart across one or more generations. Perhaps there is a friend, a former teacher, a coach, a mentor, a priest, a grandchild or even a great-uncle who will respond! And, if grace abounds, perhaps your words will deepen bonds, widen understanding and build a more loving world for those elders and young persons who will follow us.

Or perhaps you just write to write…to tell a story…to remember a season of your life.…

In eager friendship,

Ellen

P.S. Make a list of those with whom you have shared one or more letters that really matter. Or people you imagine writing to. Keep it in a safe place so you know where it is when you need it.

....

Uncle Stanley, Letter I from Worthington, Minnesota, to me at home, just before I entered the convent.

My dear Ellen,

Among the minor blessings in life there is nothing so satisfying as a big, fat letter. When written under circumstances of time and place that make vacations comfortably miserable like rainy days, sand in your bed, flies in your coffee and burning necks, it could be thrice blessed. And so it is, for ever since it came I have felt ocean spray on my face, warmth in my heart and health in my carcass. Every day I took pen in hand and began a letter which seemed to come to an abrupt end by some officium or other that demanded attention. But this last day of August for some reason or other is a Day of Decision, *a dies irae non calamitatis et miseriae, sed dies finalis et jucunda, fervida et beata,* a day that must never end until it begins to fly.

Of course we did not see enough of you when you were in Madelia. [My grandmother flew me to Minnesota for a last visit with family before I entered.] Your grandmother is possessive and a mere glimpse of her own is all that we can expect. Absurd that you should come for an hour or two even though during that time you manage to eat plenty and even take time out to enjoy Tommy's [Tom Quinn, a nephew of Uncle Stanley's] alimentary mutterings. 'Twont be thataway when you sit in the convent refectory. Your taste buds and stomach will be only of passing interest and will concern you just about as much as your hair spray.

That Ohio State interlude must have been a thing. [I did a summer National Science Foundation program there in 1966. It was a major turning point in my life and the first time I shared with my friends, my intentions to enter the convent after high school.] Something to look back to when the world was young and youth was very heaven. I'm sure that all your friends there think that you are nuts. They think that only the world has meaning and you are running away from it. They will learn gradually that life has no meaning whatsoever except the meaning one puts into it. The search for meaning is inside one and to have found it so surely at eighteen is a special gift of God. Happy are the pure of heart, for they shall see God. At the same time this is what makes this severance so difficult for your parents and your friends to bear—you contributed to the meaning of their lives for them in great part and they think that life will be less meaningful for them. They simply do not comprehend that you have got hold of heaven by the hems and that you will not let go. That this is when and where I, Ellen, grow up, make my decision, commit myself to a life and a course of action that will give full meaning to all I am, all I stand for, all I aspire to, or hope for in the end.

It does not seem much in this day and age when so many who have walked this way are finding out that religious life holds no meaning for them and they dash out in vain pursuit of some will o' the wisp that can't possibly be what they expect. I think all who have left religious life are they who when young did not have the courage to do so because of pride or fear to deflate the pride of others. Last Sunday one of our girls was in Church who has been in the convent six years. "She liked everything but she was not satisfied," her father said to me. But I didn't think she should have gone in the first place and I am sure nobody advised her to go. It's easy enough to make a mistake when young and choose the wrong road. But there is no reason to stay on Highway 30 when you should be on Highway 16. Even so nowadays there are all kinds of maps to guide one and the best one is spread out on the floor and you on your knees pointing out the way with your mind and heart.

You are right. There is no place under heaven so revealing of character than travel. That is why O'Toole and I always go together. We travel easily. I may be difficult to travel with and I don't do well with even some of my friends. But Fagan or O'Toole [both seminary classmates, Msgr. John Fagan, who lived on Long Island New York, and Msg. James J. O'Toole who lived in Toledo, Ohio,] and I never have any difficulties and we can talk for hours on end. Even this summer we spent at least two weeks doing nothing but talking. I couldn't do anything else as I did not move with ease, play with ease, eat or drink with ease. So there was just talk and some days it was a mighty spate of verbiage, I assure you. So I can see that it was good for all of you to be together this summer because never again will they all be so carefree and/or even free.

I am all for a friendlier America. A wave to a passer-by ought to light a glow, dim maybe, but authentic in no matter how grumpy a hide. But it needs more than that. A wave is not a commitment. It could be nothing more than a good breakfast sitting tranquilly in a stomach that beautifully functions. But if one could exploit a feeling of well-being to embrace those that stand stock-still, have nothing, that can't be seen against a dark background, make one regurgitate due to odor, language, disease—then we might well have caught the secret of the fourth man [the Good Samaritan] who went down from Jerusalem to Jericho. The world makes me sick as now constituted. It seems dreadfully hard, hard-boiled, tough minded, willing to destroy so much to save what seems so little. Six million Jews incinerated so that all will be gemutlich over one's schnapps. Twenty million Negroes…will they be incinerated too?

I wish I could oil paint. I can't draw a straight line. I was born lacking so many gifts. In Chicago a few weeks ago I bought three oils that I dote on. Another, a French girl or boy for the office and a still life—a bottle and breakfast stuff for our common room downstairs. They cost a pretty penny but I had to pay for them myself, as I wouldn't dare charge the parish for them.

You will be off on the tenth [September 10, 1967, entrance day,] I understand. The day is already upon us. So much to do, even to experience, before one goes. There are all those brothers and sisters whom one would like to see grow up. Imagine time molding a lad like Joey [8 at the time] into a whole man. Fascinating. But one must go. I go with you all the way. I will talk to you in chapel, on the grounds, in recreation, when all is still and you're in bed and God is close or maybe far away. You will be permitted to write me, I think. Any rule that would prevent you should be abrogated. And I will write and pray.

God bless you, my dear.

Affectionately,
Fr. S

P.S. It flies today.

On Getting Mail

"After all home is where the heart is and it is hard to carry your heart with you bag and baggage when you move to a new place."
—Uncle Stanley, letter 4

"I write an enormous number of letters…
If you send letters you receive letters."
—Msgr. J. Stanley Hale from the *Worthington Globe*

𝒟ear One dear,

Even with a very busy schedule of prayer, chores and college classes, that first month til visiting Sunday in the convent seemed to last half-a-year...and mail mattered more than almost anything. A tangible connection to a wider world, each piece of mail was a treasure! Of course, it helped to encourage incoming mail if one sent mail to others and had a steady supply of stamps! An active correspondence with my parents, three or four high school friends, my grandmother, Uncle Stanley and my seven siblings made for pretty regular incoming mail. The drawings that came regularly from my two youngest siblings who could not yet write were especially precious.

Doyle Family: Seated: Mary Kay, Jeanie, Ellen with Amy on her lap, Barry; Standing: Dad, Mom, Sarah, Joe, Tim; Cincinnati, Ohio, September 1967, Entrance Day.

On good-weather days letters were distributed after lunch on a long walk to the end of the tree-lined front lane. On rainy days, mail was placed on our personal bookshelves in the twelve-foot tall cherry cabinets in the novitiate. Incoming letters were slit open to symbolize that it was possible that they were read by the Novice Mistress, though I never knew of that happening. It was a symbolic reminder that no one could carry on a double life, I suppose. From the earliest convent days, I remember reading Uncle Stanley's letters aloud to the whole group and it wasn't long before everyone claimed him as their own uncle, with some writing to him directly.

Just this week I asked a young clerk where I got my watch battery replaced if watches were going out of style with people her age. She replied quickly, "No, they are coming back! If you wait long enough, everything comes back!" I then asked, "And what about mail? (I knew that she knew I meant snail mail, hand-delivered by a postal worker.) Is that coming back too?" Her face lit up and she said, "Yes, indeed! I just got a real post card from my friend in Florida!"

Not too long ago, I snail-mailed each of my siblings a packet of their letters I had saved from when they were children and young adults writing to me, their big sister. They were thrilled to read their child-thoughts and to see their younger handwriting. And how cheap the postage was! Their letters, one said, would be passed down to their own children.

Gotta run… More later.…

Expectantly,

Ellen

P.S. Do you remember your first letter? Perhaps written to or from camp or college? Or perhaps to or from an early sweetheart and passed along in a classroom with snickers and rolling eyes? What do you remember about it?

....

Letter 4 from Worthington, Minnesota

My dear Ellen,

It is seldom I have the chance to answer two letters in one fell swoop. Usually I am on the alert to get off an answer before another missive comes but this time you forestalled me. I aimed my last letter for Thanksgiving Day as I thought maybe visions of home-trussed fowl and cranberry sauce might foul up the day for you. It did leave you a little fey, I see. But that is to be expected and if you were a new bride in Tenderfoot, Montana, you would experience the same depression. After all home is where the heart was and it is hard to carry your heart with you bag and baggage when you move to a new place. It takes time and often an oversized moving van that could be compared to an oversized spirit of dedication. Usually it is impossible to find these oversize spirits. Generally we have to be content with a small size that needs a lot of nourishing and maybe some moisture wrapped in a handkerchief to make it grow. And it takes time too.

Time is an amazing instrument in the hands of the living God. Just think how long it took Him to make the world. He is far from finished. Or think how long it took Him before He intervened in history and then only with a tentative croaking voice: Abraham, Abraham. And then later on, too magisterial, I suppose, to go Himself, He sent one of His swifties by the name of Gabriel, to sneak up on good decent, common folk like Zachariah and Mary to scare the living daylights out of them and to promise impossible things. He is still doing the same thing with girls by the names of Ellen and Mary Ann. He doesn't send a fine strapping angel but an idea that grows and grows until it begins to make sense. One's heart becomes involved and the meaning of one's life unfolds and courage is found to share the knowledge with others and at long last a start has been made. It is like falling in love....

The trek of the Doyles to Minnesota for Christmas with Grandma will be good for everybody. All the nuances of this move I think I know and appreciate and so do you. I will not get to see them until after Christmas but then we will have them down here and give them a good day. So their attempt to fill up any empty place in their lives will be sympathetically understood. Christmas is a stinker for the bereft. A feast of love, THE feast of love, it has been a hard day for the lad who had to stay behind to mind the sheep. Whether this feeble analogy refers to them or you I do not choose to say. But I remember when I was twenty and five thousand miles from home and Christmas came round. I was moved to self-pity but a fellow came to my room (Archbishop Marty O'Connor) and held forth on the terrific spirit of the bag-Christmas. (We were the bag—short for bacarozzi—a dirty little insect whose name the Socialists applied to the seminarians.) I began to lift up my head and to take notice. And soon the music started and I began to march—I have been marching ever since. There have been days of course when you couldn't hear the tune but faintly, when there was no rhythm in your soul or your feet wouldn't track, but the flags were flying and you knew where to go. But that girl, that postulant, who came to see you and to talk when you yourself were in the doldrums, wasn't that one of those fantastic non-sequiturs that God thinks up to smooth our path? One can talk oneself right out into the daylight of God's lovely world when we are pouring it out for the good of others. She was God-sent....

The reason St. John did not record the Eucharist is that it was a going concern by the time he got around to writing his Gospel. You must know it must have been in the year 90AD. So he wrote that magnificent sixth chapter on the promise. I don't know why the very human things found in the bible should be "unbelievable" to you. Sarah was not only laughing but she was laughing in derision: "What do these young fellows know about women—after all I am way past me time." (She was Irish, you know!) The young men, (angels all, I suppose, Cherubim, Seraphim or Thrones) came back with a snappy answer: Well, you don't know anything about God. With him MISSION IMPOSSIBLE.

It is not good to have novitiates crazy about one, enough to scare the living daylights out of a man like me. And it is better at times to have in one's imagination a colossal image than to have to face reality. So let us keep the darlings in the dark. (Not bad alliteration, that.)....

Have a holy, happy Christmas, my dear. And God bless you.

Affectionately

Uncle Stanley

In the Season of Spring

....

*Excerpt from an interview with Msgr. J. Stanley Hale
in the* Worthington Globe, *page B10, Saturday, May 22, 1982*

I write an enormous number of letters. Almost every morning I spend time on my letters. I write to my nephews and nieces. Friends. You don't want to talk to yourself. So put it on paper. Talk to someone that way. Writing letters is stimulating, rewarding. It keeps you thinking about things. It fills time in a meaningful way. If you send letters you receive letters. There is a reward. And when you receive letters you learn things, you get new ideas. My mother wrote to every one of us every week. There were four boys and four girls. We all got our letters. And then of course we had to reply. That was the understanding. My mother was a good letter-writer. It was she who got us all in the habit. My mother taught school; she taught for her father in Ireland. And she was an excellent speller. There was one odd thing, the only word I know that my mother ever spelled wrong. She always spelled 'news' with a 'k' — 'k–n–e–w–s'. I don't know why that was. None of us ever said anything about it. We never corrected her.

On Writing Machines and Cyberspace

"Before I start I must tell you that I had to reread this in order to see exactly what matters I had covered. What I found was my usual spate of typing mistakes, a letter missing, two letters transposed, a verb not properly ended—all the result of my magnificent mechanical ability which sends my right forefinger all the way to P when it should stop at O, or hits the R when I should go as far as E...."

—Uncle Stanley, letter 86

*D*ear One,

We did not have a typewriter in our house the whole time I was growing up. And only the girls planning to be secretaries in my high school were permitted to sign up for typing classes. So, since I was college-bound, alas, I missed out. (Why they thought college-bound students would not need to know how to type was beyond me.) So my letter-writing (and term-paper-writing) started out with a black ink pen and cursive. And although my handwriting has changed over the years, I still write notecards and rare long letters by hand, sometimes on special paper. But typically, I hunt and peck on my laptop and cellphone using just two fingers. I've gotten pretty good at it, whether for work, play or keeping in touch with my dears by email or text or Facebook messaging. I must confess though that I am not yet a Twitterer.

Uncle Stanley nearly always used an electric typewriter for his letters, even when away from home. From what I could tell, he could type three single-spaced pages in an hour or so. I picture him zipping away, with thoughts and love pouring through his fingertips without a pause. As he got older and his eyesight began to fail, he often did battle with the ps and qs and the space bar and apologized, even as he noted that I could probably understand his intent. I think he would like Twitter though. And delight in sending short messages on Facebook for special occasions. And send astute political and church commentary, forwarding ones that had intellectual merit. And share almost-daily literary quotes from his vast storehouse to all his nieces, who of course, would be set up as a group!

Long letters are a thing of antiquity, I know. And I am not sure that I will live long enough to witness a resurgence. Yet one of my nephews fell in love through long e-mail letters to and from his sweetheart who lived at a distance. After establishing a meaningful relationship, they eventually talked on the phone, met face-to-face and married. His teenaged daughters oblige me by cordially answering my snail and email notes, texts, and Facebook messages, all of which I keep brief.

I'm wondering though about you. And where your words live in the world. And who treasures them. And who replies, if not within seconds, at least eventually. And what circumstances prompt you to want to put your thoughts into the written word, instead of risking them falling into oblivion via the phone or a virtual rendezvous. And what machines you use.

Cordially,

Ellen

P.S. Write a letter. Send it (with a special postage stamp) or thrust it into cyberspace (for free). Watch for a reply.

....

Letter 86 sent to me in St. Pete Beach, Florida where I was on vacation.

Dear Ellen dear,

Your letter came only yesterday and you have been in St. Petersburg a whole week already so, I hasten to get you a letter to remind you that I love you and to tell you a thing that you did not know when you wrote and possibly do not know yet although your grandmother said that she would call you. You know that I was in the hospital since Memorial Day with a monitor on to see whether the good doctor could come up with a medicament that would even out my pulse beat. By Friday he was ready to dismiss as he thought he had it and I believe he has, but that morning he had to come in to say that he had receive a call from Vivian that Al was dead in Palm Beach. I had talked with him every day I was in the hospital as he seemed very much concerned. It was hard to understand him as his voice gave out and was inclined to thicken but Thursday night at six he called and with tears said: "I wish I could do something for you." I answered him that I wished I could do something for him as he seemed to need it more. He passed away in his sleep at 6:00 AM Friday morning....

...The weather is really oppressive, very hot and high humidity, just the very kind of day I must bury myself behind the barricade of my air-conditioner-which-at this moment has me thoroughly beleaguered with my typewriter way out in the middle of the room away from the slip-stream of cold air that noisily proclaims it is saving my life.

Yesterday as I was beating out letter to Winnie O'Reilly, an old angel from Dublin, I went out the fridge to see what I could forage for supper that needed to be thawed out. I found almost everything thawed out. I went into a panic, and began to climb walls, hit projections, curse fate and carry on like a man suffering from dementia precox—just like I always do when something mechanical goes wrong. And the reason for my unreasonableness is, I think, that I have to face up for the Nth time that only God is great, only God is love, only God can be relied on and that all else is fallible, changeable, unreliable, even masochistic. Except my Ellen of course. She is something special. The very thought of her warms my soul and wraps me in rapture and cotton-wool....

(Just here on Saturday afternoon I was interrupted by visitors one after the other. I resume on Monday morning but am sorry I didn't get it into the mail sooner...)

But much has happened over the week-end. Before I start I must tell you that I had to reread this in order to see exactly what matters I had covered. What I found was my usual spate of typing mistakes, a letter missing, two letters transposed, a verb not properly ended—all the result of my magnificent mechanical ability which sends my right forefinger all the way to P when it should stop at O, or hits the R when I should go as far as E. But you are smart and can interpret my sighs, marks and traces of intelligence. Of course you don't know the number of P's I have erased since I began this letter. I put it down to my eyesight which is not so good as it was. But between you and me it is because of my senility. On the other hand, I, looking back, must have been senile all my life....

...I woke up this morning betimes and worked myself up to this salvific minute when I can re-establish a communion with your spirit, knowing as I do that you are reclining on a beach, quiet and peaceful, while beautiful thoughts chase themselves across the avenues of your mind—the noise of the bathers is but background music for your flights of fancy...So often do I catch myself thinking of you thinking. The thoughts you put on paper so often uproot me and make me envious that I am not tuned into the recorder so I could be carried along with you. I feel that it must be an adventure for angels and how they must flap their wings in ecstasy as they carry them up to God. You give so much to each, to all your fellow-dears, to every task assigned, to every operation, plan and ½urpose (Reach for an O and I get a P; Reach for a P and I get ½)...In a word you are a love that arrived in time's nick to keep me young, to fasten my mind on God, since I must follow you) to keep all the flags flying. Every day is a parade and you furnish all the music. I can hear your drum-thump this very minute and I believe it says: I love you. I hope above the sound of the surf you can hear my echoing drum and if Anne's conversation is too insistent tell her to shush for a minute so you can hear that I love you so very dearly. The only way out of this entanglement I can see plainly is to lose ourselves in God. We can safely follow His drum, I think, for it has the same sound as our own: To Him be glory and honor and praise.

My best to Anne, the dear person, and her parents. I will continue this when you return to BC.

God bless, dear Ellen.

Love,

Uncle Stanley

On the Ghosts of Christmas

"A cold continued to plague me, many interruptions, football games and a writer's cramp that I just couldn't overcome. Too many cards (300) and messages of all kinds wore me out before Christmas and I came to resent a pen in my hand...."
—Uncle Stanley, letter 62

"Hear me!' cried the Ghost. 'My time is nearly gone."
—From *A Christmas Carol*, Stave 1, by Charles Dickens

Dear One dear,

When I was in my twenties, Christmas Day was filled with encounters with all my primary communities: my immediate family, my Ursuline Community, the Maher family who adopted me when my own family moved from Ohio to North Carolina. All the Christmas cards had been written and sent and most of them received. And now it was face-to-face or phone time. The written word was set aside at least until after New Year's.

On a recent Christmas Eve when I was alone, I picked up one of Uncle Stanley's gifts from long, long ago: the red pocket-sized copy of Dickens' Christmas Stories, too old to even have a printing date. I carefully turned the brittle pages to "A Christmas Carol." Although I did not get through Stave One of this "Ghost Story of Christmas" before turning off my bedside lamp, I was already hooked. Not having read it from the source until now, I had relied instead on made-for-TV specials that bring the ghostly images to life.

Somehow I am now old enough to want to be with Scrooge over the dark winter weeks and days ahead. I want to companion him on his terrify-

Doyle Family: on the floor: Barry, Amy, Sarah; Sitting in chairs: Jeanie, Joe, Tim, Dad, Mom, Ellen, Mary Kay, Cincinnati, Ohio, January 1968.

ing adventures into Christmas Past, Present and Future with his three guiding ghosts, to learn from him and ache with him. I want to pay attention to the Scrooge in me, the part that holds back and counts up and chooses a solitary way at times.

What I could not have known as my letters from Uncle Stanley were coming to an end was that he would address my 1984 Christmas card but forget to include the usual letter. He did not even remember to sign it. On some level I knew this would be my last Christmas card from him. It was a ghost of a letter actually, which merely held two handwritten words: "Dear Ellen...."

I was heartbroken at the time. Yet, what more could I wish for for Christmas but that? Someone who called me Dear. Always.

Peace to you, dear friend, throughout the year that lies ahead for you,

Ellen

P.S. Which one of Dickens' three Ghosts haunts you most: The Ghost of Christmas Past, The Ghost of Christmas Present, The Ghost of Christmas Yet to Come? What are you learning from that benign but perhaps terrifying Spirit? Write it a note of thanks.

....

Letter 62

My dear Ellen,

Now and then I stick my nose into my steaming kettle and breathe; then I walk over to my desk and consider a crossword for an elusive fit; after that a cup of coffee or a lozenge. (Lozenge is a lovely word that is dying a lingering death; on occasions such as this I try to revive it.) But now I have taken my pen in hand, opened up my word hoard, summoned my faculties, and will try to put together a few vagrant thoughts that in one way or another will express my love for you. I find it is much stronger than usual at Christmas but this is natural enough since Love Itself occupies the scene and manifests itself whenever I lift my eyes—such as into a bulging refrigerator… (I never before realized that a refrigerator, that cold, frigid, impressive, occupier of kitchens, could be such a strong symbol of love. But if you opened it and saw all the meat, the steaks, the chickens, the roasts, the cookies, banana cakes, jellies, pickles, that scarcely permit you to open the doors, you would grasp what I mean.)

Then there are the poinsettias, the two-foot Christmas tree beautifully adorned, the single yellow rose (from a young mother of five who worries about me), the bottles containing not medicine, not pop, nor anything so banal as a non-lethal substance, the candies, nuts, carts. There isn't a false note anywhere—from the Advent wreath to the crib scene!

And people poured in here for three days in such profusion that I didn't have time for lunch. I never offered them anything but coffee, Port, Sherry, or Brandy. After all I know, any Christmas etiquette—God's gifts—must be available when people come in from the cold, the generous snow, the silvered trees and the whole fantasy land that has made this Christmas memorable...

January 3

What happened? A whole week had gone by since I penned the first two pages! A cold that continued to plague me, many interruptions, football games and a writer's cramp that I just couldn't overcome. Too many cards (300) and messages of all kinds wore me out before Christmas and I came to resent a pen in my hand. I know it is a benevolent despot but a despot nevertheless and never so much a despot than when one's conscience is involved and shaking you to get busy and write to these people! You promised, so get busy! The spalpeen! (That's Irish for rascal!)

...Do you know my spiritual life has gone kaput!? I can't meditate or keep my mind on God long enough to catch His attention. But I do manage to gloat over the Christmas scene and even to preach about it in a way I think that is not monkish or sentimental! Sunday & New Year's Day I thought I did fairly well. What I need is more spiritual input and one can't get that out of the new *Saturday Evening Post* or *Sports Illustrated*. But actually I have done very little reading. It seems incredible since I am in every night and the only television I watch is the football games. My mind darts around from one thing to another picking up this item and laying down that—and in the intervals, I work crosswords—and these instead of getting easier are getting harder and take more time. It may be because of a failing memory—or at least a failure to concentrate. Maybe it's boredom....

Yesterday at 4:00 PM

I escaped and went down to a nursing home and played a game of gin with a man. Since he bought a new deck of cards five weeks ago I have beaten him every time. And so it was yesterday! When I came home Charles was in my living room toasting his toes and drinking coffee I keep hot. He was on his way back from Fairmont full of beans and very happy over all the work he has done this past month. He will not be out here long! Sister Mary Willette came in about 9:00. She had been skating. I gave her some Port to warm her up. So it goes!

I wish you the best possible New Year full of delights and satisfactions and fulfilled hopes. I pray that Angela continue to guide and nurse you along the road of holiness. I pray you have the joy of your friends and that peace fills your heart.

Uncle Stanley

On Ordinary Time

> "This year you are faced with the hum-drum, the ordinary, the boring, the same personalities now stripped of their secrets, the routine, the liturgical round, the feeling that you are not living up to your capacity, the mind lying somewhat fallow and the imagination stifled by the same landscape."
> —Uncle Stanley, letter 18

𝒟ear One,

Of what are the days of our lives woven? Impatiently waiting for word from a loved one? Reading a good book, brand new and recommended by a friend or one that is read and reread every year? Rattling around in the kitchen over a harvest of tomatoes, peaches, beans?

I've come to recognize grace in ordinary time. Today, my graced ordinary-time experience would include watching the Super Blood Wolf Moon set outside my kitchen window into the bare black branches standing guard over yesterday's clean white snow. And the lunar eclipse I missed because it was too cold to go outside after a bedtime bath and a bowl of hot homemade soup. And the frustration of having double scheduled myself for two meetings set for 11 AM on Thursday. (I imagine a day when perhaps bilocation will be possible!) Not sure what grace is there, but it has something to do with noticing what is happening in the universe, and humbly admitting my ever-ready tendency to overwork.

Last week, a friend sent me her original watercolor painting on a five by seven thank you card that holds Mary Oliver's words: "…never hurry through the world but walk slowly, and bow often." (From "When I Am Among the Trees" in *Thirst* by Mary Oliver.) This longtime favorite mantra has already stopped me dead in my tracks maybe five or seven times today and it is just 10:15 AM!

My hurrying keeps me from paying attention. From being present to the ordinary, like the warm bran muffin with raisins and pecans I had for breakfast. From noticing little miracles, like two early messages from a colleague in London and one in Italy, working out the details of our week's work together. The mantra/painting sits in my prayer space reminding me, inviting me, challenging me.…

Two of the delights of ordinary-time letter writing are the salutation and the closing, both opportunities to connect in both whimsical and tender ways. Uncle Stanley was a master of both. As he was at painting a captivating picture of his own graced ordinary time. And noticing my own.

Ellen

P.S. A small set of possible writing prompts for Ordinary Time (but always trust yourself to choose your own, to write what comes…):

- Make a list of five to seven ordinary moments from today and share one or two of them with a friend or soul mate (along with what they meant to you, maybe).

- Remember a favorite book (or recipe or poem) from childhood (or later) and write what stirs in you when you remember it.
- Share a "walk slowly, bow often" moment with someone you care about.

....

Letter 18 from Worthington, Minnesota

My dear Ellen Doyle, Sister and Brother in the Lord…

I just boiled the coffee away again.

The reason-because I just came back from the school and the principal said that one of her teachers is just too hard on the children and that the parents are up in arms and what shall I do. I fielded that one and came back to the house and turned up the coffee and came in here to begin a letter to you. Then a minister called up and I had to look up a reference for him and when I came to the odor coffee filled the whole house. But you can see that my conscience is stricken-the very thought of having received four letters since last I wrote almost makes me drool, also blanch. But I must say to you in extenuation (that means to diminish the fault to a mere blob) that I have been literally pasted to the wall, like a notice of the bubonic plague, with involvement in many comings and goings.

There is the matter of all this thinking and discussion over the Community Unit Plans that embrace the whole area of the diocese. Naturally our particular plan involves only three parishes. But from a simple explanation of what might or could, it developed into a hassle where a preemptory tone began to bound off a super-sonic satellite of recalcitrance. Since this explains everything to you I will go on to the next item that purloined the time ordinarily dedicated to you alone.

This was the installation of a new bookkeeping system for school and convent only-beginning not as of now or January 1, 1969, but last July 1 which entailed the marriage of separate and distinct accounts into one, holy, catholic set of books that will finally produce after a period of gestation, morning-even afternoon sickness, mathematical vomitings, severe headaches, rejection of Father-founder back to the ancestor that created the double-entry system, a viable, healthy, even crowing creature, crept the COST PER CHILD.

I deplore the bookkeeping end of pastoral activity in any case, or I should say, in every case. I am not good at it, spend too much time at it and consider my greatest enemies Receipts and Disbursements. Had I loved it I might still be filling shelves at Hale's Super-Valu. To escape from it I entered the priesthood. And now look at what has happened in my old age. "Father, knows exactly how this should go." So a willing red-head by the sad name of Delores and Sister Lalande who has to mesh her account into the whole and I meet and meet and meet for hours, days and into the second week. But I must say the accouchement took place at 12:30 yesterday afternoon and there was finally born-cesarean-a lusty infant of the business world. But Father's infallibility is shattered, his patience suspected, his language deplored. But it was worth it. My humanity is vindicated, my ego inflated, my satisfaction complete…

But let us talk about you. High time, you say. Especially a word about that last ebullient note that came to my desk yesterday. Fifteen minutes of sheer bliss! That it should mean so much to you gives one an inkling of the great sacrifice and the great struggle that goes on in your maturing soul. The sheer grim courage to give oneself to God, the sheer grim sacrifice required is coming home to you more fully in this year of *Alice in the Looking Glass*. Last year it was sheer bliss to be learning everything, surprise after surprise and the sheer joy of freedom to do exactly what you wanted to do. This year you are faced with the hum-drum, the ordinary, the boring, the same personalities now stripped of their secrets, the routine, the liturgical round, the feeling that you are not living up to your capacity, the mind lying somewhat fallow and the imagination stifled by the same landscape. This is the year of courage, the deep plumbing into the depths of your being for the reserves necessary to go on, sometimes-not-always-the-dark night. Euphoria only now and then, like fifteen minutes in the home lot. [Except for rare reasons we could not go home during the novitiate. But one Sunday while we were in the neighborhood of my family's home, I convince my car-mates that it would not be against the rules if we just stopped by and stayed in the driveway for a brief greeting. Euphoric indeed!]

On the other hand, a lovely lady, aged thirty-two, whispered to me last night, pray for me. Today she would go again to find out whether that thing in her back was a muscle spasm or the recurrence of that cancer that all but took her life last Christmas. She smiled. She is brave. She has five children, the oldest nine. She too has given herself to God… "I love Him very much but He seems to be awfully possessive."

You certainly have some honeys for friends. Where could they be met up with except there. Even if they can't stay on a horse, ride a goat, swim a creek, climb ladders, your Sandy and Carol are perfect dears. Every bone in my body ached out of sympathy for Sandy. I know the agony she went through as five years ago I broke my bloomin' back too. I am glad she is doing much better, but tell her to fix a landing net when she goes a-laddering in the future.

Have a lovely Thanksgiving. Eat great gobs of stuff and keep on whispering thanks. I'll probably call YOU just before twelve if I can get through to you. For some reason or other you are very difficult to get—I mean the Ursulines of Brown County. Even so it is worth the effort.

Your grandmother will be in Cincinnati, she says. No doubt you will be seeing her. She really has been looking fine this past year. She handles widowhood with a sparkle I did not expect. In this case blessed be the name of Bridge.

One of my girlfriends, married to a wormy Lutheran, immature boy, with five children, just called me up from the hospital to wave at me…

As for you, sweet lady, who is trying to be holy, meaningful (sic) even, a Sister-star, God bless,

Uncle Stanley

Seeking Another Way

On Travel

> "What an adventure!"
> —Uncle Stanley, letter 2

> "The world is a book and those who do
> not travel read only one page."
> —Attributed to St. Augustine, with some doubt about its source.

Dear One,

My first letter home that first month in the convent included excited anticipation of our big adventure! The whole novitiate was invited to go to Expo 67 in Montreal, Canada with the boarding school students! My first time out of the country, a whole new land and a whole new life before me! The trip from Cincinnati to St. Martin to enter the Ursulines of Brown County had just been the beginning!

    Entrance Day had been on one of those spectacular weekends in early September when the days cling to summer and the nights are crisp preambles of fall. A strange but exciting in-between season for new beginnings and inevitable losses. Our ten-passenger station wagon was filled that day with Mom, Dad and the eight of us. I had a window seat, always the privilege of the oldest. My Dad's Navy footlocker was tied to the car's roof and held the simple clothing on the list of things to bring and a few supplies. It hadn't occurred to me that day that I would miss anyone. Even little Amy and Sarah (Amy was three and Sarah six) didn't pull at my heart, which by then, was so focused on my new life that nothing could distract me, not even Mom's dark sunglasses hiding her tears. I was ready to go! Ready for the adventure ahead!

My next BIG travel experience was fourteen years later: a move to Chicago to serve as Assistant Principal of Lourdes High School. In many ways it was like leaving home all over again. It took nearly three years to get over the homesickness, to make life-long friends, and to love ethnic restaurants and listening in on conversations in languages I could not understand. But during those Chicago years I made my way to Minnesota to visit Uncle Stanley several times, the trip being several hours closer than from Cincinnati. My last trip was in April of 1985 for my great-aunt Sister Julia's 90th birthday, the last time I would see Uncle Stanley face-to-face. Then twelve years after Uncle Stanley died my closest friend Anne and I planned the BIGGEST of road trips: from Cincinnati to Oregon, for a sabbatical that would provide the foundation of the rest of my life. We would visit Uncle Stanley's church and grave in Worthington, Minnesota, on the way. And a year later we visited cousins in Ireland that Uncle Stanley had connected me with before he died.

Visits with my family in North Carolina have always held a priority for my travel, with my favorite activity just being with them, on the beach, in the mountains, in each one's home. Uncle Stanley went to Wilmington, North Carolina, at least once and discovered the same joy, peace and fun even as he noticed our family dynamics and challenges in person!

Now, staying home is my favorite adventure. I treasure re-entering the solace of home and the dailiness of my friends' lives after a stint of national or international travel for my ministry.

Although on a recent trip to Rome, I could almost hear Uncle Stanley whisper in my ear: "I was here in this very spot in 1923 and left a part of my spirit for you, my dear Ellen dear. I've been waiting, ready to have another adventure with you, to show you places off the tour guide and discover new delights together!" (A friend once told me when I traveled overseas for the first time that I should be alert for seeing people I have already met and known…the reason being that we had already made decisions that brought us into each other's lives and so were likely to make decisions out of the same interests and values.)

So, at every corner and fountain and public square, I looked for signs of him....

I must go now...have to get a visa for my June trip to Kenya...More later.

Love,

Ellen

P.S. Write about a favorite adventure...and share it with a traveling companion.

....

Letter 2 from Worthington, Minnesota, to me at the convent,
the first letter shared with the novitiate.

My dear Ellen,

We said Mass in English this morning for the first time just to try it out and a few hours later I received a sheaf of letters from the 6th grade, of which this is a dreadful sample: 'Dear Fathers, This morning during the Canon of the Mass I knew something was different something was different in a special way gave me love and understanding of the Mass. I mean now we know the true meaning of the Mass. Fathers we are very grateful to you for many things. And now we want you to thank whoever is the head of this. (signed) Tommy'

So the English International Commission, the Liturgical Commission, Vatican II may all take a deep bow and consider it was all worthwhile!

But it does sing beautifully and I can say like Simeon: "Now, dismiss thy servant..." Although a Roman (a graduate of the North American Seminary in Rome), I always thought that the liturgy in Latin was inexcusable—as if it were magical and got its effects through sonorousness and the effects in the main were soporific. When you come to think of the absurdity years ago of translating the Latin into English missals, so that the people could "follow" the Mass, one wonders who was nuts. No voice was raised in protest, no bishop died from the cause and our beloved teacher Dante, who kept his thumb in the dyke all these years until the dam broke during Vatican II, still cannot understand what has happened to his edifice of liturgical legality that was the only possible way on God's green earth to please God. If a gesture was lost, an "Amen" unsaid or a "Let us pray" un-prayed, souls tumbled into purgatory like corn into a bin.

But by ten-thirty I was on the road to Willmar—one hundred and forty miles away with Helen by my side who was going up to visit her manic-depressive husband who has been there now for six weeks. We had lunch and after much engaging chatter arrived at the asylum at 1:00. There I greeted Barnie and gave him a carton of cigarettes. (Mystery—how can two people who have nothing spend $6.49 a week on cigarettes?) Had a cup of coffee with them and told them to have a good visit while I went to look up Alice. Alice is divorced and trying to bring up five children. Life is too difficult for her at times and she has to run into the secure structure of the asylum. But she is a good lass so I talk to her doctor at length and we agree on a plan of campaign, including another cup of coffee with Alice.

The coffee shop is where you meet all the inmates. From my parish, I met Jim, a lost lad from the Pacific who had his skin covered from top to toe with dreadful images by tattooing. He is schizophrenic and stops in periodically under an assumed name. Also Kevin who is a socio-path—a real character who wept frantically on my shoulder in the Worthington jail two weeks ago so that he could go to Willmar and become unconfused. Yesterday he did the same thing in order to get back home. His plight is laughable since it turns out that his lawyer could have got him off his sixty-day sentence in jail because of his legal rights but only his doctor can dismiss him now from Willmar. And he will not do so for a time.

I came home with Helen who is doing just fine although she too knows the insides of Willmar and other such institutions. But since her trouble came upon her she rises above her problems beautifully and is getting along just fine. I can always tell because now she comes in to see me only twice a week instead of every day.

Tomorrow I have to take off again to go to the "Mayo" Clinic of Chiropractic—which is in a little town about eighty miles from here in South Dakota. The town is Canastota and believe it or not they are doing what the Mayo Clinic couldn't do and that is to bring my shoulder back into decent use. I was besieged by a member of the parish, Doctor Gordon Smith, who begged me to go out there and finally took me there himself. He had worked on my arm for six weeks but thought that Dr. Ortmann could do immeasurably better. And he certainly has in three sessions. So, live and learn.

Such side roads of life are like convents fulfilling a need and pumping rivers of health into the mainstream of existence. Nobody dares to calculate the good they accomplish and few care to have their attention drawn to it. Why do you want to go there? Why do you want to work there? Why do you wish to bury yourself? But isn't a "flower girl in a Hippie land" also buried, fulfilling herself where all the action is, where the boys are? "But one is as bad as the other," says the conformist. "And why can't people be comfortable and conform and be nice?" Because some are born hungry or more hungry than others. And they are hungry for God and they seek him in fantastic places following their here and now conscience. Or they see the problem in a long-range, over-all picture and see the means and also the end. And the wise ones go directly to the source instead of through the by-ways of a never-never land that can't possibly satisfy hunger. Hamlet was right when he needled Ophelia to get to a nunnery since she was seeking love and fulfillment and he knew darn well she wouldn't be able to find it in him. He couldn't even fulfill himself.

Of course nobody expected you to find yourself by way on Expo-67. But what a genius thought it up! An excellent way to wear away homesickness and to soothe the abrasive qualities of companions. Travel reveals all weakness I have always said. (Like an oracle!) And after a week of Expo a group such as yours would have a common theme to talk about, a common experience to revel in. Expo could serve as the curtain, the veil of the cloister. Behind this veil we proceed to work out our destiny with whatever aptitudes and competences and motivations we possess. It ought to be a ball. To learn all the means to serve, love God. What an adventure! Especially in this age when the Church is demanding an entirely new person, a new outlook and a new method, to win the world for Christ or even to make him relevant. (A sticky word.) Out of some background, some monastery, some convent—some home—must come the colossal figure that will take the Church by the hand and guide it through the maze of our electric age....

I have to go now... but I love you in your rare moods. You actually can fall in love with life and rise to ecstasy in the contemplation of sheer goodness. Goodness is what God is, of course. Goodness and Power and Strength and Wisdom and Love. Only in him are all to be found. In others only one and seldom two. That is why you are trying to seize all at one fell swoop like a hungry lion who would devour the whole carcass of God.

Go slowly and do not get constipated less you lose the taste.

Affectionately,

Uncle Stanley

On Secrets

"Words dazzle and deceive because they are mimed by the face.
But black words on a white page are the soul laid bare."
—From *Une Vie* by Guy de Maupassant

IN THE SEASON OF SPRING

> "You are a deep one in many ways and the red line of reserve—
> no farther please—lies well below the level of dialogue or what
> you could share with another."
> —Uncle Stanley, letter 10

*D*ear One,

I clearly remember feeling "seen" and "exposed" in ways I was not completely comfortable with when I received Uncle Stanley's letter #10, in June 1968. Still eighteen years old and in the convent just nine months, I was a virgin and had not yet fallen in love. But we were focusing on chastity in our novitiate lessons and I obviously shared something about that experience in the letter I wrote to Uncle Stanley. Nothing escaped his loving, wise, probing response. I do not know what hint of trust, what glimpse of my inner soul I laid bare in my letter that month.

It would take many years, much study and mostly, the experience of falling in love, before I discovered and understood something of Angela's vision of "sacred virginity" in the 16th century context of her Rule, and its profound relevance for our time. Mary-Cabrini Durkin, a member of the Company of Saint Ursula, explores the many meanings of virginity. The one I savor more than any other is her musing about "consecrated celibacy," that "expresses a way of life which does not depend on a physical condition or any previous sexual experience or lack thereof. Rather, it speaks of commitment and implies the One to whom consecration is made, a gift of body, heart and spirit, of our power to love and to give life." (From *Angela Merici's Journey of the Heart* by Mary-Cabrini Durkin, Woven Word Press.)

Uncle Stanley loved me as a girl, not an angel and he recognized my "secrets" almost without my speaking of them. We never spoke of sex or the vow of chastity after this one brief exchange. But grace sustained us both through deep friendship not only with each other and others, without us ever compromising our vows and our one true Love in the God who called us into being and to whom we each gave our whole selves. It was a secret we shared.

I wish I could see your face, hear your voice, know what you are thinking as I write these words. But until we cross over into a life beyond this one, I must be patient and just wonder about your own secrets.

With wonder,

Ellen

P.S. Write about a secret still sleeping in your mind, your heart. Keep it private, or perhaps not.

....

Letter 10 from Worthington, Minnesota

My dear Ellen,

Idly I idle. The engine is just turning over. Gas tank all but empty, scarcely any spark. The heat is fever; the humidity just this side of a downpour. Unlike you we would go singing in the rain should it rain. So little of it have we had that we pray every Sunday for just another half-inch to force the corn to start reaching for the clouds. We are content for small favors but they must be liquid. We do not worry about not getting enough for, "never was it known…" But we like to have it delivered on the dot and not have it stew around waiting for the Lord to make up his mind. But wait we must. And we grow restive and resentful and angry and violent and we pick up paving stones and heave them at His image like the man next door or a poor professor or even at the President of the University or a man, twice-imaged, being baptized, like the current [Ted] Kennedy.

But as I say, I sit here spinning my wheels. It is very hot as I have said and would like to repeat. (It is impossible in all books since *Rain*, which was written way back in the twenties to convey a mood without bringing in the weather.) Whether weather makes the mood or mood makes the weather, all I am trying to do is convey the precise temper of a man—with no sense of guilt or obligation—that is moved by love alone to write a letter to a cherished niece who is concerned as far as one can judge about only one thing in the world and that is: When is that bloody swimming pool going to be finished? Just now I took a second gander at your letter and I am moved to forgive you because there seem to be two swimming pools you are concerned about, one at the Convent and the other at home. Two seems to be just one too many for a mere aspirant but of course a novice can handle two. And I am delighted to hear that you will soon be a novice.

The above seems pretty silly but it is approaching the silly season which is the time between 85 and 95 degrees. And today we seem to be anticipating a little. Forgive me.

Any remark I make with regard to Father Foley's session on chastity may be out of order. I don't know whether you have a hang-up on chastity or a hang-up on talking about it. I think it is the latter. You are a deep one in many ways and the red line of reserve—no farther please—lies well below the level of dialogue or what you could share with another. I think this would be true if you were married. One could only catch rare glimpses of the profound secret of Ellen Doyle. At all events I am willing to wager that you added very little to the discussion and when you did it probably took the form of not disclosing the secret that is you, for, shall we say, the enlightenment of others. You are your own person—with a great capacity for love and affection towards others so long as the citadel remains inviolable. But I am glad that out of it there developed some food for thought. I am inclined to go on about this at least from this angle that a whole girl does not offer this thing or that thing to God but the whole girl if she is going to become an Ursuline, her total love. And Julianna of Norwich, bless her medieval soul, may say, "Love is in the Wille" but it is in the body too, in the blood and muscles and nervous system, in the whole girl who is no angel. A fond uncle might call her an angel but she is no angel—she's a girl.

I hope your foot appointment turned out happy. Everybody was glad to see you, to bless your foot that brought you home, I suppose, with Sarah and Amy taking off your shoe, chortling gleefully over the blessed happenstance. I wondered as I considered the fact that a magnificent thought in the mind could never bring about such a liturgical procession to the Lares and Penates, no matter how vividly expressed, a lousy corn on your little toe could accomplish it. What a piece of work we are!

During these two weeks of CCD you will be very busy and almost totally indifferent to any letter that might turn up; so I thought to leave it in the typewriter with the hope that some stray thought might be added. But I decided I had better put it in the mail. After all there are all kinds of paper, envelopes and stamps that could be used for further writings.

God bless you my dear.

Uncle Stanley

P.S. I put this announcement in the church bulletin this week, in CAPITAL letters for effect: CONCENTRATE ON PAYING UP YOUR CHURCH SUPPORT, UP-TO-DATE BY JULY 1. WE WILL SEND OUT NOTICES THEN TO ALL THOSE WHO NEVER SEEM TO WORRY MUCH ABOUT IT. START WORRYING....

On Inner Rooms and Other Sacred Places

"And how that night about 2:30 AM George came into my room dreadfully ill and how I stayed with him until morning and then got a doctor for him. And how he was hospitalized and died the day after New Year's. And how we sang a *Te Deum* on hearing the news because we were in that Christmas mood

> and heaven was just next door. He was a lovely chap
> but of course God knew that too."
> —Uncle Stanley, letter 50

*D*ear One,

Not too very long ago, I listened to a young colleague of mine describe how much she treasured praying privately before the Blessed Sacrament. She relished turning off her phone (even the signal), letting go of the distractions that usually follow her wherever she goes, and giving herself over to silence in the presence of her God.

I found such a place beneath the giant sequoia tree in front of the Monastery of the Angels in Mt. Angel, Oregon, and in the hermitage called Joy at Cedars of Peace in Nerinx, Kentucky. One year, I simply took one word to my silent prayer: STAY. And breathed. And waited. And trusted.

At the time I am writing this, we are all sequestered at home because of the Covid-19 pandemic. We are in our tenth week. Instead of airplanes (on which I often find a sacred silent space once we take off) I sit in my chair, protecting three hours each morning for uninterrupted time. I sometimes walk slowly and bow. It is a great grace, this time and space in the midst of so much suffering. I breathe. I wait. I trust.

So many ask, what are we learning from this pandemic? What to want to continue or keep afterwards? I want to keep my inner room, my mornings. And eight days next week in a hermitage at Cedars of Peace are beckoning....

Sending virtual greetings and care to you!

Ellen

P.S. Do you have a sacred inner room somewhere? How long since you have been there, breathing, waiting, trusting?

Letter 50

My dear Mary Ellen,

I am in the exactly right mood. I think it came about suddenly after I spent an hour cleaning up the top of my desk. After every cotton-picking item was disposed of, it came down to your letter only in all its shining invitatory splendor. So why not insert a piece of paper in the machine and take off and show my love for my dear and favorite nieceSister. I have exactly one hour, if not disturbed, before I have to take communions off to two Nursing Homes and visit another where I will end up, please God, playing a game of rummy with a man who sits waiting for somebody to sit down and deal the cards. It is a busy day here as the CCD classes are going on and all priests in the neighborhood as well as Sisters and lay folk are immersed in Young America trying to make a dent for God. I am above that sort of thing, relegated to this superior level by virtue of a decree that says: All deaf people should stop trying to make dents for God lest they get dented themselves by hidden slingshots, cross-bows, arbalests by inattentive spalpeens who are fed up to the teeth with a world without dialogue. Thus I am free to write and need only the mood.

I've been having trouble still and the doc thinks I should dash off to Rochester for tests that cannot be made here. Like sticking a long spoon down your throat: a search for a stone in the pancreas or adjacent territory. He said he was going to get an appointment there Sunday but I have heard nothing. I feel as full of beans as a snake after he got shut in a can of pork and beans by mistake. But suddenly I am in difficulties and in real pain in my chest. It is an odd way for the Lord to let me know that the gravy train is passing by slow but sure and the foothills of the Rockies are in sight. It is an amusing interlude in some ways. It has all the glamour of a change of scenery in an old time Opera House playing Tempest and Sunshine. One emotes, one is bored, one dashes to the bathroom for more Maalox. And if that doesn't work he surreptitiously takes out of his pocket the secret phial containing the stuff that works every time. It, however, is not to be used except in dire straits. Too hard on the kidneys! So I really cannot say what will come of this adventure with God and his decrees. I can only let him have his way with me. I certainly am not going to burn and bluster like King Hezekiah at my age. Blessed is the Name of the Lord.

7:00 PM I was interfered with and now I continue....
In the meantime dinner has been eaten and I enjoyed it....

I loved the vocations folder. I spotted you and Sandy immediately. It is a beautiful thing and Dolores deserves at least an eagle for it. Sandy always outlines her background so definitely and incisively with her bony face and the part in her hair. She looks so much like what she is that one always feels when looking at a picture of her like saying, "Praise be Jesus Christ, Good Morning, Sister!" (This is how I was brought up-which always gave us the opportunity to seem a trifle profane while paying obeisance in the proper, Notre Dame manner.) You are doing the talking in your picture and it must have been a profound statement from the looks of deference of the other two... The formation that I already have sensed has taken place testifies to an undergirding that will be strong enough to meet any of the coming tests. One can accept the idea that at seventeen or eighteen one might well run to escape the challenge of life that one seems unready for. And all the way to a convent. But one is bound to grow and the challenge is still there and the decision has to be made. In the meantime face-to-face confrontation with our Lord opens up vistas that prove so inviting that one becomes unwilling to accept anything less. You all look to me as if the challenge has already been met, the decision already made.

You may be sure that I will pray for you and the nieces with all my heart. I hope they will not be lacerated in spirit or agonized in mind but that each may slide into the future gently, maturely, courageously. Just think of a child's world without these three and yourself ready to show them the wonders of the Lord! Empty it would be. Empty...

You are of course right about Christmas. It is a bad time to visit... But I recall Christmas time in the seminary. It was glorious and the thought of being anywhere else was simply repulsive. The atmosphere of love and good fellowship and the feel of the proximity of the Child in the crib as a center of prayer, of mirth, of song, of understanding, was simply overwhelming. I recall vividly George Fletcher and I hanging out the back end of a tram corning in from a trip to Tre Fontane Abbey and St. Paul outside the Walls in Rome the very day after Christmas, chewing tobacco that somebody got for Christmas and spitting great globules of juice all over the footsteps of the martyrs, confessors, Virgins and saints, and even taking a shot at Keats tomb at the foot of the Caius Cestius pyramid as we rolled on by. And how that night about 2:30 AM George came into my room dreadfully ill and how I stayed with him until morning and then got a doctor for him. And how he was hospitalized and died the day after New Year's. [This could very well have been a death due to the global pandemic flu of 1918.] And how we sang a *Te Deum* on hearing the news because we were in that Christmas mood and heaven was just next door. He was a lovely chap but of course God knew that too.

Gee, I have done wonders. Almost three pages. I am almost as good as Stephen. But it has been a long time since I wrote and I must make up for it. Say hello to all my nieces and remember that I love you very much and hope that one of these days you will show me your new abode amongst the stars. Or what is astronomy for?

God bless,

Uncle Stanley

Where Silence Reigns and Solace Lies

> "We are SENT to use a current word that usually ends there and names not the destination. But we know where the destination is—deep, deep down at the very core of our being where dwells the One we seek where silence reigns, where solace lies and all nerve-ends meet."
> —Uncle Stanley, letter 69

> "Be still and know that I am God."
> —Psalm 46

> "There is in all things an inexhaustible sweetness and purity, a silence that is a fount of action and joy. It rises up in wordless gentleness and flows out to me from the unseen roots of all created being, welcoming me tenderly, saluting me with indescribable humility."
> —From *Hagia Sophia* by Thomas Merton

*D*ear One,

On the second day in the convent the routine of silent breakfasts began. That morning it was almost as if all seven of my younger brothers and sisters were sitting in the chairs where the other novices and postulants sat at our big square table. I could picture them peeling their bananas, drinking their milk, elbowing one another just for the fun of it, but definitely not keeping silence. Despite my efforts to hide them, tears welled up and fell into my cereal. There was solace in their saltiness. And in knowing that no one noticed.

Now, I savor silence. I seek it actively. Perhaps the thirty-day silent retreat I made in 1973 in preparation for final vows laid the foundation. Having a quilt with me to work on that summer slowed me down and helped push would-be-distractions aside. The solitude made room for my deepest desires to well up. I hope the same for you, dear One.

With love,

Ellen

P.S. Find a chair. Sit still for ten minutes. In silence. Write what wells up....

....

Letter 69, with Christmas Card

My dear,

I have been reserving you until last and suddenly it looks as if I am going to miss the boat and not get a letter to you in time for Christmas. Father Jerry Mahon was in here this morning before I finished Mass. He is the dynamic vocation director-very young with tremendous faith and enthusiasm. He thinks I am a kindred spirit and when he comes West he always stops. He has gone over to the High School to interview a prospect and will return after for lunch. Father Charles arranged the lunch at Cheevers. Then at 2:30 the Region IV priests' meeting starts down at the parish ending up with dinner and a penance service. One thing after another. So I hurried to this machine the minute Jerry got out the door to pen this love letter.

I am in the very pink of health thanks be to God. That is, I appear to be. How my pumping organs and breathing apparatus is I don't know and do not worry about. Except when I go out in the cold and can't breathe. That is an invitation to seek out a travel agency and look for the sun some place. I will stick it out until mid-January as I want to go on Retreat on the sixth. I hope this time to go to Phoenix or Sun City. Pat wants me down there after they return from Dallas and I think Al could do without me as he is confined to the house and certainly can't be in any mood to entertain.

I shall send this out to Brown County as no doubt you will be refuging there come Friday night. What do you intend to do during vacation—renew your soul in that atmosphere of mutual love and kindred spirits? All the nieces will be there and Anne and other mutual friends. The palaver will go on and the decibels will go up and you won't need any wassail bowl or can of Hudepohl to lubricate your tongues. Then there will be the solitary moments, the walk in the woods, all bundled up, and your thoughts churning with the wonders of the Lord.

Great is our Faith and filling for the mind and the heart and whether we are pursuing a family going down to Bethlehem or a wild man howling in the wilderness telling us to straighten things out and end this crooked business, or some solemn looking VIPs rocking on a camel's back or shepherds lazy-bodied over their sheep or even some heavenly visitants caroling to the music of the spheres, it echoes, re-echoes, reverberates in our bosom. We are SENT to use a current word that usually ends there and names not the destination. But we know where the destination is—deep, deep down at the very core of our being where dwells the One we seek where silence reigns, where solace lies and all nerve-ends meet. So fill your soul with Christmas, breathe it in, rub it on your skin, eat and drink it, in fact get drunk with it. It is the Lord.

And God bless you for being you and my well-loved niece and friend. Live long in the land and bless it with your goodness and kindness and the spirit of your being. Hold fast to what you are, what you have, what you aspire to....

I love you. Merry Christmas

Uncle Stanley

On Staying Home

"I will stay home for Christmas this year…"
—Uncle Stanley, letter 110

*D*ear One,

Masks, washing hands (long enough to sing the tune of "Happy Birthday," and staying home, (or at least six-feet apart) is the way through and beyond Covid-19. It kept me home for Christmas 2020. And the many months before and after.

But, if truth be told, having unscheduled days from time to time in between the busyness associated with planning and facilitating virtual meeting, is a God-send! Each one is precious with slow mornings AND afternoons, time for contemplating, stretching, reading, writing, watching and waiting. Even giving up Christmas with family and community was a small price to pay for such solitude. Surely healing, rest, and eventually herd-immunity after enough get the vaccine, will follow.

Be well. Even if stuck at home.

Ellen

P.S. I do not presume to think you like staying at home. But if you do not, do you know someone who does? And do you know what they like about it? Draw a home-sweet-home picture, compose a home-coming poem, or do something that can best be done at home. Perhaps invite one person into your home for a heart-to-heart chat and some soup. Or visit a homebound person with cookies from your oven or a favorite bakery.

IN THE SEASON OF SPRING

....

Letter 110

Sunday morning
My dear Ellen,

The furor of the Christmas preparations is over and I have come into this peace where I can stash my soul alongside your own and bask in the warmth of your quiet and your love. It has been a hectic time but I think I have done the best job ever as I received letters in return that were so kind and loving that they made me weep. Even the phone call from Shreveport last night at eleven from a former convert to wish me a Happy Christmas and to tell me that of man born of women I was his favorite. Of course he was maudlin and I had a hard time getting away from the phone. And another from Mrs. Dugan in San Diego yesterday afternoon which was overpowering as she thought I had done so much good for her family. But the best was a letter from Molly Peterson of Shakopee who protested that between their father's illness this summer in Minneapolis and my letters to him and to them, the whole family has returned to the Church never to leave it again. And then there was the call from John Fagan in a Long Island hospital to say Good-bye. His brother Father Jerry has come over from Ireland to take him home and I am sure I will never talk to him again. He is dreadfully ill and everybody is afraid of what may happen on the trip so that everybody is praying. A grace note to all this was a call to your grand-mother last evening who said that a glimmer of daylight has appeared, and she now hopes she will get home for Christmas. But you know this as you talked to her yesterday afternoon. But when I went up to see her on Tuesday she had an angry, nasty foot and was not full of cheer. Since then your father has been by and probably given her a tremendous lift... Let us hope that this is so. But I don't think she will ever travel again as she is beginning to look her age, which remember is eighty, just a little older than I.

It's a beautiful day today—the very first all week. So dismal and dark have been the days that they quickened my spirit in self-defense and moved me to do many things to pass the time and to catch up. But today is fine and after a session of football I will go down to the penance service at 3:30 and have my sins shriven. Later I will go to a wake of the fourth good man of our parish who have died in the past few months. He was fourteen when I came here and now at forty-eight leaves a family of six. His wife is not Catholic but she is a beloved friend of mine and she sent for me Friday morning to the hospital when he passed away. I was out later to hold hands with her and came to the conclusion that she will carry on, a valiant woman.

I have been overpowered by Advent. I offered up every possible prayer and rosary and Mass and itch for the Mary Inkrots and the Tim Rekers of the world but especially our diocese that young ones may find their way into the vineyard. Father Mahon is beating the bushes these three weeks and he needs all the help he can get. I expect him to turn up here next week or this. Like you, he is on the same wave-length....

My kind of rosary is catching on as I get many notices to that effect. It has become a sinecure to say. All it needs is time. Time is something you have little left over after a full day, I know, and you must be exhausted from the pre-Christmas demands on you....

I got two pinecones from your father and I have them on the bench in the window and on the telly set. They add a woodsy atmosphere to the room. I have two other plants and Mary Pat will be here Tuesday and I'll bet a dollar she will have another-just to celebrate Christmas in my bachelor place. She's a dear! I will stay home for Christmas this year....

I hope you got the frantic note I sent you a few weeks ago with the twenty in it which you were to spend frivolously. I trust your meeting with the Erie Sisters of Mercy was a love-feast for both of you. I hope all my friends there are well and up to plucking Santa Claus by the beard. Give them my best love. As for you, you have my heart right in your hand, so all I can say is I love you.

On Prayer and Holiness

"…By the way, how about learning about prayer
from Baruch, Ezechiel etc. Prayer should be all-embracing,
as wide as the sea, big with love."
—Uncle Stanley, letter 6

"The romance of the priesthood is the quest for holiness…"
—Letter 100: the article "Priests—men like other men,
beset by weaknesses," by Msgr. J. Stanley Hale, published in
The (Winona Diocesan) Courier, April 15, 1977.

"But I must emphasize the goal—the ultimate aim—is holiness."
—Excerpt of the homily Uncle Stanley gave
at my Final Vows, August 11, 1973.

"Be holy, for I am holy."
—1 Peter 1: 16

Dear One,

Uncle Stanley said more than once in letters long ago that he had regretted not praying more when he was young, not learning how to pray sooner. That it was too late to learn it once one was sick or in real need. Perhaps like

Uncle Stanley, far left, in the sanctuary of St Mary's Church, Worthington, Minnesota.

learning a language, the prayer mind-set was more agile at a younger age. And then when on the verge of "sliding down the banister into the ash-can of eternity" (his own stark image) it seemed to take so much more effort.

Somewhere, I did learn to pray, to know something of God and God's ways with me and all the others. And I am still learning. To trust my relationship with the Divine, the Holy One, the God-Who-Is-Among-Us. To be content and still in silence. My thirty-day retreat in preparation for final vows was a foundation, of course, as was my learning to love. I do not believe that one can pray if one does not know how to love, to express love with affection, to ache with the hurts of love, to receive unconditional love even in times of betrayal.

I have also come to believe that a daily spiritual practice is the life-line of prayer. Morning prayer with the readings of the day. Night examen or Evening Prayer with the psalms. Yet I still slip away from this regular rhythm on occasion. I rationalize that there is not enough time, that I do not feel like sitting in my prayer chair. I do not breathe in, breathe out, with centeredness. Instead of waiting, setting my intention, reading the scripture of the day, choosing a phrase for a mantra to guide me, journaling my intentions and questions and love-letters to God, I sit in the chair for fifteen seconds, put on my socks and begin thinking of what the day will hold. But I come back to the chair. It is too important to my soul's blood and breath and bones.

The image of Uncle Stanley's faithfulness to praying the Divine Office at least three times a day no matter how busy he was draws me back. Thankfully, God continues to be gracious and patient with me. Our imaginative, generous God invites me to discover new names and faces of the Divine and laughs as I relish the sacraments and rituals of Catholic tradition even as I hate it's frustrating and oppressive patriarchy. This is my home, the spiritual birthing place from which I have come to know that the Holy One loves me, really loves me, with a faithful magnanimity.

And of course, any practice of prayer, together with compassion, kindness, gentleness, patience, forgiveness leads, step-by-step, to holiness.

And so I end with a prayer for your well-being and intentions, that you too may be holy.

As ever,

Ellen

P.S. Do you have a favorite prayer? A prayer-practice you are using or hoping to use? Write about what draws you to prayer (or what causes you to lean away from it).

P.P.S. And what about holiness? Is that idea attractive or off-putting? Invite someone you love to coffee or have an online chat about "the joy of the pursuit" of holiness. Just do it.

....

Letter 6 from Worthington, Minnesota

Friday
My dear (Mary) Ellen,

Was not my heart burning within me when your letter came this morning with the advice, suggestion, command that it was not to be opened until St. Patrick's Day. I stood it as long as I could and then I said to myself, I said: "She has just stolen one of my tantalizing tricks. I know what I will do. I will write her a letter that she wouldn't expect me to write without getting the very latest from the conventual Front. After all that is where the war is." So I was charmed to see Snoopy waving his native flag on top of his dog house. He gave me a great lift immediately and I needed it. I had just received in the mail a summons to a Consultors [a gathering of priests called for consultation with the Bishop of Winona] meeting in Winona [where the diocesan offices were located] next week, Thursday. I was in Winona just two weeks ago getting the Bishop Heffron Award citation, given at St. Mary's College. It is a long way down there in the wintertime. One of the blessings of being in Worthington, which so may deplore, is because it is so far away from Winona. And a Consultor's meeting is not a thing that exactly fills one with joy. I have reached an age when I don't care to listen particularly. I like to do the talking. And a Consultors meeting is a monologue. At least it has been until I became a Consultor....

"The Death of Mail" happenstance [the practice of holding all incoming mail during Lent and delivering it on Easter Sunday] is a thing that has afflicted all religious since the beginning of time. I don't know whether it is Lent or simply *Puritis hiemalis* which seems to be just the opposite of "cacoethes scribendi" that afflicts all people between the eager gushing opportunism of Christmas and the dolorous explosion of Easter, but this is your first experience of the Septuagesimal disease. So when this letter is put into your lily-white hands you are to realize that it is only by a kind of holy serendipity that you are so blessed.

I must tell you that I have no vim (or vigor either) to waste on the young. I must conserve such gifts lovingly and selfishly if I am to abide at all. But maybe on the weekend of May 12 I may be able to work out something. The week before or the week after one must hie oneself to the [North American College, Rome, where Uncle Stanley was a seminarian, ordained April 3, 1926] Alumni meeting in Chicago for the good of his soul so I may be able to take advantage of a Blue Cloud Benedictine's presence (who will be here to beg) and absent myself from felicity while I take on a convent full of lions. But just maybe!....

I have an inkle that you are not getting enough sleep for your case load. Exhaustion is not to be fooled with, may your uncle tell you (your Grand-uncle—accent on the first syllable). Up to the age of fifty I got along without sleep, going to bed at midnight, reading for an hour or two, getting up at six and seldom getting a nap. Then I collapsed at the altar one fine day when Sr. Julia [his oldest sister, a member of the School Sisters of Notre Dame, Mankato, Minnesota] was here and scared her out of her linen chains and they took me off to Rochester [to the Mayo Clinic there] in an ambulance. Exhaustion, said the Truth and Consequences boys! It affected my memory, my ability to concentrate and took me a year to really rally around. I've never been the same since and am bound to go into a premature senility as you can plainly see. So watch it, girl!....

...By the way, how about learning about prayer from Baruch, Ezechiel etc. Prayer should be all-embracing, as wide as the sea, big with love—taking in LBJ (also HH, my pet) [Lynden Baines Johnson and Hubert Humphry] and the stinker in the alley—everybody with the face of Christ. Even uncles need prayers and nieces of all descriptions. Especially, nieces! And not perfunctory but demanding prayer; none of this: Thy Will Be Done stuff; (Of course, His Will is going to be done, why shouldn't it be?) But we need to shake the very teeth of God. Not that God's teeth need to be shook…but we need to shake them. Our prayers are weak because our faith is weak… So while you have twelve whole days you can give them over to prayer. What difference does it make if the devil comes along after and tempts you with sole ownership of the Museum of Modern Art? The Lord will send his angel (maybe me) to comfort you.

I have a thousand things to do and I must fly. Have some green soup for Sunday in honor of St. Patrick and in the language of Lenten Terce: "May the Lord deliver you from the snare of the hunter." And the unkind word.

Affectionately,

Uncle Stanley

....

The article "Priests—men like other men, beset by weaknesses", by Msgr. J. Stanley Hale, published in The (Winona Diocesan) Courier, *April 15, 1977.*

A few weeks ago I was waiting for my doctor in Minneapolis when I fell into talk with a Campfire girl just ten years old. She had a tin can with a hole in it, some cookies to exchange for any offering and a slight lisp. When we completed the exchange satisfactory for both of us, she asked, "Are you a priest?" I wanted to shout, "Of course I am a priest and have been for over fifty years." I asked in turn, "Are you a Catholic?" "Uh-huh! 'N I made my first confession yesterday."

She made her first confession yesterday, and to a priest of course. It was one of the unbelievable gifts the Church empowered him with on that grace-filled day of his ordination. Along with the power to preach the Good News, to make the Eucharist, to minister the sacraments. To do all these he had spent years in preparation. They were the goal of his striving, the realization of his dream. And they are the signs of his professional competence. But they do not make the priest.

A priest is a very special person. He has been singled out, summoned from among men, as Aaron was, to be a representative before God. And above all to be another Christ. *Alter Christus* was the phrase our spiritual directors always used. That is to put on the image of Christ, to make Christ the center of his life, the very ground of his being. In a word, to be holy.

A priest is ordained by his bishop, but holiness depends on himself and his cooperation with grace. He is a man like other men, beset with weaknesses, and they can be many—pride, greed, sensuality, anger, gluttony, envy, sloth. From these ordination does not liberate. Up to then the idealism of youth minimized the temper of the conflict but now the issue is joined. And it is too late to retreat.

We blithely jumped into the struggle as if everything depended on ourselves. Disillusion came all too slowly as we were busy with many things that appeared to depend on our energy, our personality, our charm. So busy were we that habits of meditation and prayer formed—in the seminary gradually melted in the furor of the daily tasks and the demands we permitted to possess our lives. There came a time even when the daily Mass, the Divine Office and, we might add, the annual retreat, were supposed to provide all the spiritual energy we needed for the fray.

After all, we were doing God's work and we did not shirk it. Many tasks were assigned to us and we welcomed them all and fulfilled them all. Our self-satisfaction was complete. What is more, we congratulated ourselves on our wise choice of motion as opposed to contemplation. This seemed to be what the world we lived in called for. For some reason or other we identified our way of life with St. John Bosco, who had been immersed in so many activities. We ignored the fact that his activity was rooted in contemplation. Doubts would assail us in a moment of illumination, and we would make a special effort to turn about and retrace our steps. But that didn't last long. The light twinkled out and we were back on the treadmill of self-expression, of seeking fulfillment, of being meaningful for others.

How we managed to keep our equilibrium at all with such a secular outlook is a mystery of God's grace. Did we falter, and some faltered and wandered off into the wasteland. But we put down to the rigor of the game and turned quickly to the Mercy Seat. Looking back at the outcome of all the tests that we pray God daily to deliver us from makes one suck in his breath and pause in wonder at the mystery of God's goodness and the fidelity of His love.

To trace the mystery of that love through one's life is one of the delights of old age. Also a supreme adventure in humility. Sometimes the pattern is so intricate, or so breathtaking that one stands in awe. Instances stand out like beacons on the way. What would anyone make of the words of a young prophetess, bless her, who had the audacity to tell you after the close of a truly magnificent class lecture: "You think you know everything. I think you're conceited." Angry would you be? Quick to retaliate in kind? Or would it suddenly dawn on you that if that was the image you were presenting to the world you were a far cry from being another Christ? One can only shudder as you recall that conceited is precisely what Christ called the Pharisees.

In all this there is no mention of the world that impinged itself on one's life. The depression, the wars, the social explosions we must leave to another day. Even Vatican II and its aftermath, where we are inclined to pause, we pass over. Suffice to say that we greeted it with open mind.

The romance of the priesthood is the quest for holiness. There is nothing on land or sea "worth the wear of winning" than to put on the image of Jesus Christ, our Lord. That it has escaped us so far does not lessen the joy of the pursuit.

Besides, we are young yet.

....

Excerpt of the homily Uncle Stanley gave at my Final Vows, August 11, 1973.

Most Reverend Archbishop Bernardin, Fathers, Sisters, our newly professed, relatives and friends. I would like to say to the Most Reverend Archbishop that I am somewhat embarrassed over pre-empting his role as teacher this morning. So I would like to tell him: they all call me Uncle! Thus I had to come down and participate in this happy day in some fashion or other…

So it is no wonder we are filled with joy today. It spills down from the ramparts of heaven. And indeed, if the angels are enraptured when one sinner turns to the lord, they would be properly "turned on" to use our language at its best—when four young maids give response to his call and say—with hearts in their mouths—"Speak Lord, your servant is listening."

It appears that it is the humanity of Jesus that first attracts people. There is a deep hunger in us that responds to him. What were John and Andrew and Cephas searching for wandering about the Jordon that they did not find in the Baptizer? That stranger that John hailed by a wonderful word "The Lamb of God:" one glance from Him did it, that one look that could draw a soul out of the night of sin and fulfill its every longing, that voice whose cry could raise the dead or comfort the possessed—They heard for the first time: 'Whom do you seek?' He said. They didn't know what to say. But they had to go with Him, they couldn't let him pass by. 'Rabbi, where do you live?' they managed. 'Come and see.' 'Come and see!'

It is to this invitation that you are responding so eagerly this morning. You too must find out! But I must emphasize the goal—the ultimate aim—is holiness. It will take all the time that is available. It demands a full commitment, a total gift, a true espousal, a complete engagement of mind and heart and soul. Not for a time only—as so many are able to interpret these words nowadays—but in perpetuity, forever, until death unites you to your Beloved.

Each one of you has many gifts. You can all teach, for instance. But you are gifted in many other ways. Because of these gifts, Our Lord has chosen you to go forth and bear much fruit that will endure. Therefore the development of these gifts is essential. It could be that with a certain overemphasis on their pursuit you could be led into by bypaths that would interfere with the main purpose of your lives. But that could be true of any other relationship or interest. This seems to be the common malaise of our times—if not of every time—our uncanny habit of allowing the lesser thing to consume our energy and dominate our lives.

As an antidote to this tendency, you have Angela. You recall how she knew from her youth that she was to found an order of women in Brescia. Not for a moment did she forget it. *But* she had to become holy first—a finely-tempered instrument. For sixty-one years she pursued her primary aim until she almost had to be forced to do what people would call her 'life's work"—the founding of the Company of Saint Ursula. In five years she was dead. But her Company flourished like the apostolic Church because the founder was holy and her companions were holy.

So what you do with your gifts, my dear friends, no doubt will be much but it will be nothing compared with what you do with your holiness.

Dolores, Sandy, Ellen, Carol, a few minutes ago, Sister Ann Catherine called you by name in the name of the Lord. You answered: 'Lord, you called me—Speak, your servant is listening.' And what does He say, but 'Be holy, be holy, for I am holy.'

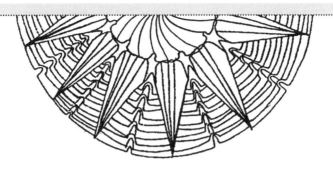

The Letters in Four Seasons
In the Season of Summer

Summer sings of independence and dances with discovery. Sudden storms surprise and new roles and relationships take root. My own summer season of life spans nearly two decades of learning and teaching. After leaving home for a wider world, I found my life's work and several soul-mates. Entering the Seminary and studying in Rome when just a teenager, Uncle Stanley spent his summer seasons connecting with family in Ireland and discovering literature, art and music in Europe. Summer solitude had its precious time and places for both of us, bearing fruit in silence, in our quests for meaning and in our love of community. We were both in our mid-twenties when we made life commitments that neither of us ever questioned even as the world around us changed in ways we could never have imagined. Uncle Stanley came out of summer between the two Great Wars and modeled a renewed priesthood after Vatican II. I emerged from the Novitiate after Vietnam and paved the way with others for new forms of consecrated life. Summer equipped both of us with the trust that with good friends, clear purpose, and God at the center of our beings, our life experience would prepare us for the autumn harvest that would follow.

Loving & Befriending

ON FAST FRIENDS AND LONG LOVES

"Your loving letter really touched me so much
that I had to take time out to thank God that
he introduced you into my life at a time to make
my old age a happy time just to enjoy your love,
your youthful enthusiasm, and *joie de vivre*."
—Uncle Stanley, letter 55

"And a youth said, Speak to us of Friendship.
And he answered, saying: Your friend is your needs answered…
And when he is silent your heart ceases not to listen
to his heart; …And let there be no purpose
in friendship save the deepening of the spirit…"
—From *The Prophet* by Kahlil Gibran

"It is simply beyond my thinking this summer
that I might see you. I was beginning to think that
only through letters and the phone would I be able
to communicate with you anymore."
—Uncle Stanley, letter 156

"and in a mystery to be
(when time from time shall set us free)
forgetting me, remember me."
—From "in time of daffodils(who know)"
in *Selected Poems* by E. E. Cummings

Seated L-R: Ellen, Uncle Stanley, Sandy; Standing: Dolores, Carol, St. Martin, Ohio, August 1973, Final Vows.

*D*ear One,

I have always been one to have a few close friends. Even now, with so many ways to stay in touch, I lean toward a select few.

When we arrived at the convent over an hour late there were warm-hearted hugs from the Sisters along with questions about whether we had had any car trouble or gotten lost. I hadn't met the three others who were entering with me: Dolores, Carol and Sandy (the other three "nieces" Uncle Stanley would come to love. (Dolores Lindemann, Carol Hauser and Sandy Bates all entered the Ursulines that day as well and we became close friends with one another.) We all had a quick snack of lemonade and cookies and then everyone was politely thanked and invited to come back again in a month for Sunday visiting hours. And that was how my new life (and friendships) at the convent began.

Uncle Stanley had hundreds of friends, though just a few close ones, including parish families, city officials, priests, nieces.

Twenty years later, while I was living and teaching at Ursuline Academy in Cincinnati, Uncle Stanley visited regularly. He came to be friends with Cecilia Huber, Phyllis Kemper, Kathy Green, Anne Maureen Maher, Mary Inkrot, and Jill Leonard besides the other three who entered with me. All were welcomed into his love and affection and some became correspondents with him.

It wasn't until after Uncle Stanley died that I lost my four closest friends to death, within a few short years. And it wasn't until after my own experience of loss that I had a glimpse of the experience of loss in the generation or two ahead of me. I vividly remember coming home from my senior retreat on a high, wanting to share the experience with my mother but finding her, then just in her mid-thirties, sobbing over the loss of her closest friend to cancer after just weeks since the diagnosis. And the letters from Uncle Stanley telling of the death of Frs. O'Toole, Fagan, and Matthews, and Marylyn Adel, dear Marylyn Adel, all dear friends of his.

I have come to count you, dear One, as friend, precious in this last stage of life.

Be well. Be safe. Be a true friend.

Ellen

P.S. Remember the finding (and perhaps the losing) of a dear friend. Write what comes....

DEAR UNCLE STANLEY

....

Letter 55 sent to me at Colombiere Retreat Center, Clarkston, Michigan, where I was on a thirty-day retreat, in preparation for final vows

My dear,

Your loving letter really touched me so much that I had to take time out to thank God that he introduced you into my life at a time to make my old age a happy time just to enjoy your love, your youthful enthusiasm, and *joie de vivre*. I find myself in complete harmony with all you think and do. I relive my own days of discovering the world, its meaning, my own identity. What I like especially about your approach to life is your special devotion to your friends—how close you are to them, how dependent and how their well-being so definitely touches your own. In this, of course, you are very vulnerable is you are laying yourself open to many disappointments, because others do fail us not because they turn away but because they fail to understand or even be aware of our need. It is here I think you ought to concentrate during this retreat—simply the cause of your generous ability to respond to them—that friends, circumstances, are gifts. Not that our Lord is an Indian-giver but he gave them to you for your growth and to teach greater dependence on Him and may withdraw some gift—only to give you a greater one in return. So open up your heart—be vulnerable, love at will, but be ready to forfeit it if it is the will of the tremendous Lover.

In this I was very unlike you. I always thought of myself never in relationship to others. It took me a long time to discover other people. Even to this day I am afraid of rejection and therefore am wary of identifying with others. You have helped me immensely in this, my dear, and I thank you for it.

I really never had anything to offer you. But you poured yourself into my life like a goblet of wine or champagne thrown at a vessel to be launched. Thank God that I had the sense to respond. And now I am more dependent on you than you could ever be on me. And moreover, you shared your friends with me and I feel so very comfortable, so loving, with them. I would like to be able to show them all my love in some way but how could one do that? But they must sense it—as I do their love.

I recall the days when I was making critical decisions too. From some bright angel there came the wisdom that made the whole thing easy—and that was this, that after years of practical, everyday preparation for my ordination, it was no time now to wrestle with the devil or any other diversionary will-of-the-wisp. After all I liked doing what I was doing; I was there to prepare for the priesthood. I had qualms over the years and selfish, sensual, worldly, migratory longings but I had never done anything about them. So, why now, should I make a big thing of a decision that could be BIG in my mind only because of my pride—that being a priest deserved a wrestling match, a dramatic catch-as-catch-can encounter with the powers of darkness or daylight, the attraction of the fateful hours or the noon-day devil. Romantically the moon is the Big Cheese but it was only the reflection of the light. I thought I possessed the light.

It is so long ago, but as I look back—stupid as I have been and so slow to learn what other could have been! And now that it is all but over and time is running out, I can only thank God for all his graces and blessings and regret only that I didn't learn faster and had to be shown so often.

It is now time for dinner. I have bought a lovely writing desk but prefer to sit here in my sunny breakfast nook. I dine at the rectory but breakfast and lunch here. I shall have a daiquiri (that is to celebrate our lovely conversation—I feel that close), then a kidney bean sandwich (which I read about in my cookbook) and some strawberries for dessert. I picked them yesterday in Heron Lake, cleaned a few quarts (they are for you when you come) and kept more for breakfast food, lunch and whenever. I love them. (I am apt to break out with them!)

2:00 PM

My kidney bean sandwich was a huge success and my nap a lullaby. Soon Father Mathews will be in to carry me off someplace. I called him up as he has not been feeling well and invited him in for a trip. It is sunny, cool-ish —but we may go down to Okoboji and absorb what warmth we can get. Too bad we can't play golf as yet, it would be an ideal day for it. So I'll write until he comes and then mail what is written and a add something later.

Yes, I think I'll go down to Long Island early enough to return by way of Toledo where I'll stay a few days with O'Toole. Then drop down to Cincinnati a few days before the 11th! Then I'll be freed for whatever—even to take you home with me. But mind, my dear, you and I will spend most of the time hereabouts. You may visit your grandmother a small piece!

At my Mass this morning you and Dolores and Sandy and Carol loom large. Tomorrow I'll say Mass for yourselves alone. I must get busy with my sermon. I'll have to get it ready before I take off on the Eastern trek. Then when you choose your readings I'll force the two together…

Father Matthews is here. God bless now. I'll write soon. My dearest love and all my prayers.

Affectionately,

Uncle Stanley

....

Letter 156

𝓜y dear Ellen,

Although I talked to you yesterday you won't mind, will you, if I talk to you again? It is a dreary day, dark and dismal, but very little rain when we need inches of it. I just ate a sandwich—pork with mayonnaise and a glass of iced tea. I broke one of my nice plates as it slipped out of my hand. I will watch the baseball game and later go down to the Church and say a few prayers as I am storming heaven for another good friend of mine, Jeanne Sprader, who lives in Menominee, Wisconsin… She has a wonderful husband, Al, and four quite grown children. At least the baby, Mary, just graduated from High School. Then I will stop in and see how the Adels are doing. They returned from the Black Hills on Wednesday. The sparkle of course is gone out of the house but they are certainly putting on a brave front. But when Valerie and Cheryl go away to school it may be different. But it is amazing to note how those two girls have matured in but a few weeks. Lucky they have an angel for a papa….

…I am beginning to be excited about seeing you and hope that nothing comes up that will prevent it. It is simply beyond my thinking this summer that I might see you. I was beginning to think that only through letters and the phone would I be able to communicate with you anymore. And here I am on the verge of a good hug and a whole eyeful of the sight of you. Just looking at you has always been such a pleasure for me as if I had created you, like God, who ALWAYS WAS DELIGHTED WITH THE WORKS OF HIS HANDS. (Don't mind my capitals—I just got my finger in the wrong place). As for the thought just expressed, it sounds a bit blasphemous but is only meant to convey your preciousness to me. So blessed am I in my old age with very dear people! [He lists many in this letter: Sr. Mary Willette, Sr. Kathy Green, Sr. Cecilia (aka-Ceil), Pat Forsythe, Mary Schmid, Doc Fitch, Al Molitor, Dale Krekelberg, Bill Meier, Bob Harens and Richard Adel.]

Tuesday
Yesterday was a busy day, I went down to get my ticket for Cincy. I shall leave here or from Sioux Falls about 8:00 AM and get an AMERICAN plane out of Chicago at 1:50 and arrive in Cincy at 3:53. Okay, I hope. I met a couple whom I deeply love who were on their way up to see me. So we coffeed for an hour or so downtown. I was late getting lunch but managed to get everything together by the time Father Loomis came to take me to the picnic. The salad

was a huge success and there were about sixteen present. We lingered alongside the lake until twilight amid the good talk and the camaraderie. They are a great bunch of men! Of course there is the usual number amongst us who cannot converse but can only play cards. It's the same group that go all the way to Jerusalem, Acapulco, Jamaica to play cards. What they would ever do wrecked on a desert isle without a deck of cards, I don't know. Maybe they would have to mark palm-leaves in some way....

The first page has been around the kitchen for some time now, I just now found it on the floor. Pardon the grease or dust....

I feel quite good inside today as if the Lord was blessing me. Maybe it was because I was determined to get this letter finished and off to you. When I finish it I will go out and visit a few friends, stop in at the Church to wave to Our Lord and his Mother and visit a few sick. I have some Belgian stew defrosting and will stew some cabbage as I have a new big head. After dinner Pat and I will go shopping and I will give her half the cabbage. In between times I will have you in mind and am needling the Lord to smooth your path.

Bless you now in the Name of the Lord and grow big with God. So much love.......

Uncle Stanley

On Pen Pals and Soulmates

"Anne is right about you…"
—Uncle Stanley, letter 41

"I am very happy that the trip to Erie was so satisfying and helped cement the love you and Kathy Green have

> for each other and the great lift you got from talking to her."
> —Uncle Stanley, letter 100

> "The Lord has taken Marylyn from us
> and we sit here half-crushed at the thought
> she will be with us no more. We do not understand
> this mystery of her passing any more than we
> understand the mystery of suffering."
> —Excerpts from Homily for Marylyn Adel's Vigil Service.

> "As time runs out for you in Chicago, I can imagine you
> on tester-hooks waiting to be gone. It has been
> an interesting interlude in your life—."
> —Uncle Stanley, letter 194

*D*ear Pen Pal,

Sometimes I imagine you writing me back. Like my three closest soulmate friends did when our friendships began. It was the written word that was our foundation for sharing, trusting and early friendship.

Anne was separated by about fifty miles and on the other side of the Novitiate where I still had restrictions on visiting and receiving mail (although the pony express worked fine!). She watched out for me on holidays when I was homesick and welcomed me into her family when mine moved to North Carolina.

Kathy was a five-hour drive northeast but we were united in our having made a silent thirty-day retreat together as we prepared for final vows in our separate congregations. Our friendship began in silence, continued in letters and four-years later included phone calls and visits before she moved to Cincinnati just as I was getting ready to move to Chicago.

Jane lived in Chicago where we served as co-directors of a summer final vow program for two years, just as I was moving from Chicago to

Charlotte. She lived down the street from a wonderful bookstore on N. Clark Street, Women and Children First, that had one-of-a-kind cards that suited Jane's bold, flowing handwriting, the script of an artist.

I was present at the bedsides of each of these three soulmates just before their deaths. We no longer needed words. Amazingly, the writing that began our friendships now sustains our connections these years since their passing. Our written words serve as an enduring bridge across miles, time-zones and life itself even more than at the beginning.

Peace to you, wherever you are, my friend,

Ellen

P.S. Write about (or to) a pen pal, a soulmate, someone whose suffering you know, a friend that you companioned through death.

....

Letter 41 from Worthington, Minnesota

My dear Ellen Doyle,

I shall start writing now on this day at four PM and continue until such time when I am disturbed when I shall desist until I can begin again. But I promise that this time I will be persevering, tenacious, unfaltering, not easily discouraged nor outraged by circumstances that so often compel me to tear the sheet out of the machine and throw it into the waste-basket with a spate of accompanying billingsgate that would put a dock-worker to shame. Should I have to stop I shall start again; if words won't come I will wait until they do; if my mind runs on to other things, like a pup sniffling at every bush and tree, I shall wait until it returns. In such manner I build up ego, stifle any latent impatience, abort any illegitimate nuance that might lead me astray.

Your simply dandy letter is still on my desk simply screaming for an answer. The very color of it has inflamed my eyes day after day for a whole month. The very thoughts it contains and the questions asked compel me. So I begin by saying it is a long winter and the Lord might consider a point of order. Lucky we have been to have escaped the full fury of storm after storm that struck South and North and East and left us with only flecks of snow born on speeding winds. But it has been cold, days at a time, with only occasionally a respite. The weather has been bad enough to erase from my mind completely the memory of the sun that warmed my straining carcass on the Arizona desert. I will have to think a bit about a day of nothing but sun but if you start looking for such a heaven on earth it may turn out to be heaven itself. Which gives rise to another thought.

What I have been trying to say is that I have not yet succeeded in getting to Madelia to see your grandmother. Twice we had a dinner arranged and twice I was thwarted by the weather. But maybe on Thursday I may be able to make the grade. I don't know why she left the sunny(?) South to put up with this kind of thing. But then I suppose one simply runs out of words or social exchanges and it is time to go. One's own home and one's own freedom begin to call commandingly....

That you have decided to go back to school next year ought to make everybody happy. I know that I am as this is the time for schooling and not later and not piece-meal. Wherever you are your friends do not seem to be too far away. I hope that Carol has an opportunity to go on and I hope they give Sandy what she wants. Maybe she doesn't know what she wants....

...You on the other hand are an independent person towards whom lesser mortals gravitate. Anne is right about you and I don't know what is wrong with it. The more I note your relations with others working out in time the more I believe that you are the center. But you may be right about Bert. She may well be the strong, isolated person that everyone must recognize. I pray for Bert. I hope that she finds a strong man to love. But I am afraid she will settle for some character who will do nothing but lean. If you have a chance tell her to be careful in her relationships. She is too much of a person to be used by leaners.

It took me some time to evaluate you as I really did not know what came out of the top of the can of the Doyle family. After all you had nothing but adulation from all sides. So much was expected of you. So much of WHAT, you might say. So much of whatever could possible evolve, I suppose. Nobody was going to put a pin in it but they expected you to be a conversation piece of mental success at least. When you elected the convent driven by heart (maybe) spirit (maybe) the grace of God (maybe) it deflated many bags, I think. But you have gone ahead with a gusto and spirit that has left us all (I include me) breathless. And every letter you write is simply unbelievable. You can go home and enjoy the love and affection of the family and return to your love without a hair out of place. As if this is my life, there is no other, here I stand; I must get on with it. You can talk to your mother over the phone, identify with her loneliness, her love and anticipations of emptiness as the children scatter-and go right back to doing your own thing with a gusto and abandon as if you were a prophet of the Lord and things had to be done and words said and a life lived no matter what. And when I think of all the people who have passed across the pages of your letters to me and all the relationships and the love received and expended I can only conclude that you have a BIG HEART Ellen Doyle and I love you very much....

I will call you on the phone soon. After you have had time to read this letter. I know how very busy you are but please get one off soon....

God bless and bless you.

Uncle Stanley

....

Letter 100 from Caledonia, Minnesota

𝓜y dear, dear Ellen,

It was neat to be able to find you on the phone last night just as I developed enough courage to call you at another's expense. I wanted to beat Richard Rohr to the phone and I find that I did. He said he would call you as soon as he got home. But if he is anyone like myself too many things pile up and have to be attended to before one finds the opportunity to pay attention to amenities. I do not know what I could say or add to the conversation last night. You know how he operates and what he is full of: sharing the love of God through Christ. He hammered away at it in one way or another day after day and aroused the lads to fever pitch… He is very perspicacious and knowing. What I liked about him was his devotion to his leadership group. He is with them so much and considers them as important to his message as he himself. They were a delightful group, everyone so different but so devoted to the New Jerusalem Charismatic Community. Three of them married and present without spouses indicates a view of the apostolate that got home to all. Even the Bishop couldn't believe it. He thought such a display of maturity in love was Christian indeed. He hates a display of affection in any form but was almost converted this round.…

Confirmation here tonight and we are expecting the Bishop any moment. I know that he has had a hard week because he had to confront a couple of recalcitrants which always slays him and he will come staggering in here like a soldier home from the wars and begging for peace and love. He will get it in this household. He will stay overnight although in striking distance of the parish because he always visits the classrooms when he comes like a good shepherd.

I may take off to La Crosse in the morning to get fitted for a suit of clothes which I ordered. I want to look nice on my visit in some future after-life or your happy abode. When you urge me to come I get to pawing the ground and my urge goes way beyond my reach. It looks so simple, so easy some days but then I am inclined to pause and use not my heart but my good horse-sense. Horse sense which is almost identical with the sense of doctor usually prevails. On the other hand I could get desperate should you not find a way to come hither....

I had all your intentions at heart during the week as you say you had mine... I felt your closeness, your hovering, loving presence as it was your praise of Richard Rohr that brought him to Winona finally. I am very happy that the trip to Erie was so satisfying and helped cement the love you and Kathy Green have for each other and the great lift you got from talking to her. Phyllis must have had a very happy time too. I came home to Holy Week too and was completely uplifted by the experience. I couldn't bear not being home for that week. I have to pray in my parish Church. There my spirit is at rest. This is getting long and I don't want to dominate the typewriter's use. So I will say God bless you forever and ever and ever....

Much, much love,

Uncle Stanley

....

Letter 194 from Sun City, Arizona

My dear Ellen,

Try not to disdain, chuckle, or throw up as I take my pen in hand. Since I cannot read my own writing I know that I am putting you to the test. But I had to return my machine yesterday as time ran out on it. Since I will be leaving Monday, please God, I thought I wouldn't need it anymore. But this morning I got lonesome for you and dared to think that you could put up with my screed if I were extra careful. So you can see I do the best I can. I do not hurry it. I concentrate. I proceed—

Your note astonished me that you are seeking a ministry in North Carolina! There is no doubt it will solve the matter of the summer, being close to your family, supply a much-needed vacation. As time runs out for you in Chicago, I can imagine you on tester-hooks waiting to be gone. It has been an interesting interlude in your life—I think it will be a long day before you decide again to share living space with another. But one learns about things only gradually, but one learns.

Ceil and I have become short but regular correspondents. Bless her heart and all the trials and tribulations and she has had to face up to as the dismantling of the historic Ursuline Center takes place. But it must be unsettling for all of you—as if the old home had swept away and left you half-orphans. [We had made the decision to raze the Brown County Ursuline Motherhouse and another key building there.] It puts each person more on her own to make her own way in the world while clinging to the past and Blessed Angela—

My social life is more active than usual during this last week—luncheons, dinners, farewells, and the retracing of steps over the old sidewalks were I have come to know every crack, the depth of every curb, the shape of every palm tree, the spine of every cactus, the smell of every rose. At the Sun Bowl two blocks down the street is a very riot of roses perfuming the air like a battle of Caron's "Christmas Night" which is the only bottle of perfume I ever possessed—given to me at Grasse, France by Bill Bogus for my mother.

I'm also making the rounds of my pubs where I enter and sit making out a crossword in the dim light and drinking a Bud. It is a special kind of life made to order by a good God for an eighty-five-year-old!! The other day I met one John Lynch, a former editor of a New York paper who recognized me as a priest in my disguise. Smart cookie—we had a great visit!!

We will not say Mass until noon. But I'll say goodbye for now.

Love,

Uncle Stanley

P.S. Isn't this the week your mother is in Cincinnati on retreat?

....

Excerpts from Homily for Marylyn Adel's Vigil Service:

The Lord has taken Marylyn from us and we sit here half-crushed at the thought she will be with us no more. We do not understand this mystery of her passing any more than we understand the mystery of suffering. That suffering can have infinite value we know from the sufferings and death of Christ, our Lord. When endured in Faith, its value must be immense extending far beyond the good of the sufferer and effecting the lives of many.

Marylyn had an insight about suffering from the very beginning that sprung from her deep faith and identification with our Lord Jesus whom she always approached with open hands. When I wanted to know exactly what happened in Sioux Falls she dropped in one night to explain how her experiences seemed to coincide with the vagaries of MS although the doctors were reluctant to call it MS. Before she left I asked her did you say, "Why Me?" "I did not," she answered, "I know better than that as I am no better than the next, but I did say, "Why Now?" Even the "Why Now" disappeared as she came to realize what the Lord was demanding of her. So she set about making her offering on behalf of her loved ones, counselling, encouraging, strengthening each. So she left us; that bright and shining personality will be with us no longer. But our memories will be full of her and we will ever recall her ways, her interests, her activities.

She had so many talents and was lavish with all of them.

We think of her first as a home-maker. We across the street were really astonished at the grace-filled atmosphere of the Adel home. We got to know the whole family, (as Richard would say: the whole kit and caboodle), intimately from their earliest years and we marked the steps, the gaiety, the joy that went into every change and success and triumph of each one of them.

We enjoyed being in on the refurbishing of the house as it was accomplished, room by room, floor by floor over the years. And admired the plans and ideas as they flowed out of that fertile brain, so artistic and so practical. When finished she swept out into the garden, formalizing it, and built a gazebo, I think, just to have a gazebo. And how she loved to frame and hang on the walls the rules she lived by and taught her children. I often thought that had she met Moses at the foot of Sinai when he came down with the ten commandments she would immediately have had a copy made and hung on the wall. And she would have kept them too....

Her outside interests were many: The Church first I think—and especially the choir, with her soprano voice soaring to the skies and giving joy to many as she loved and praised her God. If a director was needed and for a time one was often needed she would take over and do an expert job. If at times she would appear in a frightful white wig it only added to the general merriment on a Wednesday night's practice.

Then there was the school. From the beginning she watched over and guided the progress of each child keenly aware of the needs of each. With the graduation of Valerie it was time to go to work as College expenses tended to soar. She had no difficulty finding a job. Married to a coach, she followed every team, rejoicing in their success, bewailing defeats, cheering on her own lads and girls as they in turn took their place among the athletes. When Victoria's team needed a coach for volleyball, she volunteered thereby reaching the very apogee of her ambition and joining her husband as a member of the coachs' confraternity.

Socially conscious, her heart bled for people who were not getting a fair deal. When to the surprise of the City Fathers a swimming pool was voted by the people and nothing was done she sent off a blistering letter to the Globe that galvanized them into action. Thus we have a facility that delights the young and old these hot and humid days.

Then, of course, she was a Christian. How she lived her Faith and how she gloried in it as each child received the waters of Baptism, made its first Communion and was Confirmed. Each stage on the road was the occasion of a happy, joyful celebration. And how she rejoiced as Richard and Valerie were chosen to read the scriptures, Clifford and Conrad to serve the Mass, and she was bursting with pride when Richard was asked to be a distributor of holy communion at Mass. And how excited she must have been when Richard was able to bring her Holy Communion from Holy Rosary Church every morning as she battled for her life in Minneapolis. To receive her Lord from the hands of her beloved was very heaven!

And finally, she was a friend. One had only to ring the doorbell of her house and you were met by a smile and a greeting that were irresistible and you were made to feel thrice welcome as if you had come to bestow a benediction. The family gathered about and when the time came to depart you were accompanied to the door by the whole family whose courtesy towards the departing guest was an open invitation to come again. All of you knew Marylyn and she was your friend. Each one of you knows what she meant to you. As for me it was something very special....

On Many Marys

> "Mary Ann the latecomer has already substituted me
> for a grandmother. But the responsibility for an uncle is very
> serious, Mary Ann, and should be approached prayerfully and
> also in a gusty manner, like a Santa's Ho! Ho! Mark it, child!"
> —Uncle Stanley, letter 28

> "I shall embrace Mary Inkrot in all my prayers. I need
> another youngster to worry about and to love a bit.
> I hope she threads the needle of the future
> with deep spiritual insight."
> —Uncle Stanley, letter 76

> "And a lovely Hallmark card came from Mary Kay with
> a rampant lion cradling behind his forefeet the most blissful little
> lamb with the one word Peace on the inside. She couldn't resist
> sending it to me—which tells me more about Mary Kay
> than a thousand words. So you have some unique sisters
> coming up behind you…."
> —Uncle Stanley, letter 131

*D*ear Mary (even if your name is NOT Mary, I am pretending it is, just for a moment!),

Mary was my mother's name. Mary Catherine to be explicit in the Hale family, to distinguish her from the many other Marys in the clan. She was dear to Uncle Stanley too. Mary Pat was another niece, my mother's first cousin. Then there was Sr. Mary Julia, Uncle Stanley's oldest sister, whose real name was just plain Julia. The nuns added Mary in front, as they did to me too when I entered, to help us come to know and love

Mary the mother of Jesus. And Uncle Stanley's parish of thirty years was St. Mary, one of many in the Diocese of Winona so it had to be identified by its town, Worthington. And there was Mary Kay, my sister, Mary Ann, another Ursuline friend, and Mary Inkrot, an Ursuline Academy student who became a friend of mine and entered our community. All the Marys had a second name. Uncle Stanley loved the many Marys and wrote to many of them.

I cannot think of any name that has become as common in our day as Mary was back then. One-of-a-kind names seem to be preferable nowadays, names that are not necessarily tied to a saint or even to a known person. But there is indeed something wonderful about having a common name carried by family members and friends. And being named after someone is a gift, as I was named after my grandmother and my niece was named after me. Another thread of connection that ties one person to another in family and in friendship.

Whatever your name, I hope you love it. And feel special as a unique person no matter what.

Blessings,

Mary Ellen
(as I was called for one year in the novitiate)

P.S. Look up what your name means if you do not know that already. What qualities resonate with you and make you glad you have that name? Have you given your name to anyone or received it from someone you love?

IN THE SEASON OF SUMMER

....

Letter 28 from Worthington, Minnesota

THURSDAY NIGHT!
*D*ear Ellen Doyle Sister,

Do you prefer almond bar, mint parfait or chocolate creams? This is the question I was just asked by two demure Junior band girls as they came out of a wind-swept night, cold with flurries of snow. I set my mind to answering the question and finally gave up when I realized that they were the first pair to occupy the hall. When the second and third pair come I shall order the other two kinds. In the meantime I thought I preferred the almond bars.

This is the end of the very day that really began when the mail came this morning and there was added to the spice of life a new scribbler from the Doyle sept. It was Barry who wanted to tell me about the great Moeller team, the fact that he had received along with the team communion under both species (which made him feel a greater togetherness), the studies that made up his slate at which he was very good in the main and lousy in history. I was charmed and flattered. I immediately took my pen in hand and wrote him at length and I thought that he might be mature enough to consider the holy priesthood. That we were beginning to get down to the bare bones of the vocation that the runners were running from and a new breed of facers-up-to-life were taking their place. I didn't see any reason why he should not do so. Am I right or am I nuts and what does a boy like Barry Doyle think about?...

I just shudder when I think how close Christmas is. I have 250 cards to get out on account of my BIG HEART and the thought always freezes me until I spend a week in bed and then I have only weeks left. But this time I am going to circumvent my daemon. I am invited to spend the evening of the NINTH with Archbishop Binz (as he has time enough now to visit old friends) at a dinner, a bed and a concelebrated Mass the next morning. [Archbishop Binz had served as the Bishop of Winona before being assigned to Dubuque and then to St. Paul-Minneapolis.] I accepted although I should know better. But after all, when one gets old, deaf, sulky and bereft of invitations to first class dinners one is inclined to go. There ought to be good talk as there will be nobody there but a half-dozen contemporary Romans and reminiscence will be the piece de resistance.

O'Toole and Fagan were a tonic and we talked and talked until suddenly we were beginning to be repetitive. It was time to break up. So we broke up. Fagan left on Friday morning and O'T on Saturday morning. I came home from putting the latter on the morning plane and worked straight through for twelve hours. When I was finished I rested. Sound. I had the Bulletin to do and then a ballot for the whole slate of Church Council officers to make out, a sermon (to get up and Office to be said, good John Scholtus to anoint (whom I buried today) and a Jerusalem Bible to deliver to my favorite doctor.

Since I wrote your grandmother this afternoon after returning from Wilmont and the burial place I have been looking for your last note. It was short and accompanied a magnificent turkey done in stretch pants. I have it hanging on the Bulletin board where all can measure their tongues by. I will now take another look.

Oh for God's sake don't be so blooming servile. I'll bet you went off into the corner and felt sorry for yourself because the priests didn't notice you at the dinner for the Forty Hours. "But then basically I suppose we are all servants of the servants of God." What an utterance! I am sure you must have heaved a great sigh and went back to the dishtowel feeling like Paul VI or something!

FRIDAY

The assistants' day off… I on these occasions (and the occasion comes on Friday—like eggs and fish used to) try to get an early start on the day because it always manages to develop into a melee of the first water. So, since this letter was still sticking in the typewriter because I was side-tracked by a birthday party in our basement put on by the present convert class and never got back to it, I hasten before the deluge to finish it. You know well that under such circumstances you usually end upright quickly with, "Love, Ellen." I on the other hand always write another sentence and it is this: I was very happy to get the attached notes from Carol, Mary Ann and Sandy. Carol's card of sympathy which was bought but never sent I will send along now. In the meantime did the second edition of Phoebe become a cropper or are we going to wait interminably for the article on the Sittenbaumian Indians? I suppose she is going to blame the delay on a cyst.

I never did intend to start a second sheet. It makes too great demands on my time. You might say: What is time for except to waste on expectant nieces. But Sandy needs a word of cheer. I was going to say wisdom but she is a wise enough bird and knows all the answers herself. The questions she asks are purely rhetorical, not meant to be answered but merely seconded. I second them all. Authorities would act like persons and not like drivers of a slave ship. But she wasn't spoiled by authority, she just learned how not to be authoritarian. Which may be a valuable lesson, which many don't learn. I miss you too Sandy and I hope your back is better. Mary Ann the latecomer has already substituted me for a grandmother. But the responsibility for an uncle is very serious, Mary Ann, and should be approached prayerfully and also in a gusty manner, like a Santa's Ho! Ho! Mark it, child!

May I go now? I'm getting conscience stricken. But do please put your dear confreres to work on Michael Quinn. [Michael Quinn's body was never found. His name is listed on the Vietnam Memorial in Washington DC.] I talked to his wife again last night and she is taking his missing status gallantly. But the whole situation looks bad as no one has heard his beep. Missing over southeast Asia is like being missing on the dark side of the moon.

God Bless. Love

....

Letter 76, Monday

𝓔llen dear,

Your letter just came and while the soup heats up in the pot I shall start an answer. One never knows, does one, how or when it may end up. It was such a lovely letter, such a special treat for a bird like me, such a rare gift for anyone to receive, that it almost started the tear ducts. It was exactly the kind of letter that I knew was being written in your heart all these weeks of silence. As you say, we read each other's minds and so sensitive are our antennae that we really don't have to depend on words any more. Not for a moment would I doubt your love, would I have to wait for half a year. But then of course I would want something to feed my heart on even if not my mind. It has something to do with our Lord, I think, far more than kinship....

You walked into my heart precisely at a time when I needed you badly and you simply flooded it. I remember the minute so well when you came into the room in Worthington that day when all of you came down from Madelia to visit me. Your heart was on your sleeve, an offering gift, and your smile simply was a gigantic invitation to accept you. Why you were moved to be so generous on that day I will never know. But ever since I have been totally yours. Out of whatever simplicities this came to be I do not know but as the years have gone on and I have plumbed deeper into the mystery that is Ellen dear I just simply go on howling: THANK YOU, GOD.

WEDNESDAY
Strange that I cannot finish anything anymore. I don't think that I am so busy but I can't begin anything important without being interrupted in such a way that I lose the thread and sometimes the needle....

But now that dinner is taken care of and I don't have to dig something out of the freeze nor make like a cook I ought to be able to write for the rest of the day. I notice that "Prayer is a Hunger" urges one to put down on paper one's thoughts and hammer them out the hard way lest they flit too easily, are too imprecise, reach no great depth, establish no continuity, do not discipline one's mind, leave nothing to refer to. I am almost tempted to try it but I am afraid that I would get in the habit of sending them off to you before they properly jelled or developed into any real worth. You would then be the waste basket of a thousand unconsidered trifles and not the sponge (Fr. Matthews just phoned: he's coming in.) you truly are—an absorber of the infinite. For as I read you I can see that you have been delving into books that feed your mind beautifully and you are beginning to run away from me into an inner world of your own where I won't be able to follow. So pedestrian is my pace, so plodding my steps, that I spend my days in semi-exasperation (half-mad) at my failure to tear the heart out of the simplest idea. It must be my education that is at fault or my low IQ or my life-long attempt to absorb much but nothing well. I feel that I will end up in an educational or rather, intellectual, ashcan. I will never be able to straighten out in my mind such a simple statement as, "God is Love." For even there I have to start out with something as familiar as this: "I love Ellen" and go on from there instead of starting out with, God is love and coming down to Ellen.

Friday

One way not to use stamps is not to send a letter. Just wait and accumulate words that will justify the expenditure of ten cents. Thus I am still on the same letter. This time I will start out with a family note. I am so very happy that you and Mama are getting together. For a long time she thought you were an enemy that dared do THAT to them but now time and grace are working their wonders and she is beginning to appreciate the fact that she has a prayer-child always there in the back ground and interfering in the lives of the loved ones at home, as prayer always upsets the calculations of others, and she is finding that it is good. She is becoming dependent on you now and is beginning to bless the day you were born and the day you said Yes to God. She no longer is seeking other ways of coping but has come to a peace that will change everything in the family. They should really get out of that town and into a city and an environment that would offer some response to her growing aspirations. On the other hand maybe she will manage to lead or at least plant a means in Wilmington that her friends and neighbors can find harborage in.

Tuesday

I drove up—my first venture out by myself—to Madelia, had lunch with Lester, that good and excellent man, and spent an hour and a half with Nell. She is coming along in grand fashion with her walker and awaits only the appearance of someone who is willing to help her at home before she departs. It has been a good experience. Always good comes of these things like my old friend by the pool in Bethesda. (I still don't know what happened to him but I have some doubts whether he finally made it. He seems too churlish and ungrateful.) I came home at 4:00 PM after shouting in at the new baby at Tommy's: Molly Brigid, a sweet colleen sound asleep in a crib....

    I looked up the passages of Scripture you mentioned and loved all of them. Of course I devoured the John 4 but the Deuteronomy and Matthews are much to the point and not so familiar. Isn't it amazing what a tagline will do for one at times? The word of God is the Word of God indeed, creative penetrating, scouring. If one could only be open, wide open, to it at all times, be alert when He comes, when he speaks.

> "Pause by me that footfall
> Is my gloom, after all
> Shade of his hand, outstretched caressingly?"
> —Paraphrase of "The Hound of Heaven" by Francis Thompson
> (I used to know the "Hound of Heaven" by heart and taglines intervene as I write with no sharp reference to what I am trying to say.)

A week later…

When I finished the last page, I was weary and thought I should go out and get some fresh air. It turned out to be somewhat disastrous. The minute I stepped out the door into ninety-degree heat and high humidity I began to have a queasy feeling. So I just went out to the shopping center and bought some ice cream, strawberries and had a cake frosted to serve Sister Julia, the Hodapp nuns and Fr. Paul Hodapp who were coming down on Saturday to visit me for a few hours. I met too many people out there who wanted to visit and by the time I got in the car I was ready for a Nitro. I came into the house and took one and when I felt up to it went back to the car and carried in the groceries. In a short time another angina attack came along and wouldn't go away. Izzy Smith had come in just as I took the first Nitro and by the third she called up the doctor who came running followed by an ambulance. They took me off to the intensive care unit and kept me there until Sunday but the attack passed and there was no tissue damage. As they say in medical parlance: no enzymes in the blood.

 I came home yesterday afternoon with the strict admonition NOT to go outside at all in this heat. So today Charles came along on the way to Okabogi where all the priests of the region are meeting for a swim, golf, boat-ride and cook-out. I had been planning on that for some time. But, of course, when you work up nerve enough to abandon yourself to God then suddenly realize that must include angina attacks you just don't go around feeling sorry for yourself. So I rejoice that I can stay home and take up where I left off in this letter that should have been finished long ago.…

 Since I can't wait to talk to you any longer I will call you tonight I think. Sarah and Amy won't be there I know since they will wait now until later when they can be whisked off to Minnesota at the end of their stay. But camp will be on and you probably will be sleeping out in a bag somewhere thoroughly bitten by mosquitos, those monsters that lug around all the butchers' knives.…

 …I hope you have come back from that blessed Florida relaxed and at ease and in a prayerful mood. I have been praying a lot for you as I am afraid that you are inclined to overdo—not pray over much—but work over much. I shall embrace Mary Inkrot in all my prayers. I need another youngster to worry about and to love a bit. I hope she threads the needle of the future with deep spiritual insight. I think I am in favor of girls getting off the treadmill and into a safe haven as soon as possible. A safe haven is a place to contemplate Jesus. Like that branch of the sycamore tree that Zacheus had recourse to. By the way I wonder did the Lord accost him by name as the gospel says or did he call him Shorty?

I love you.

Uncle Stanley

P.S. I've got my machine in front of the altar where the air conditioner is. Inspiring, not?

....

Letter 131 from Caledonia, Minnesota

Tuesday
My dear Ellen,

I have just eaten too much dinner and my silhouette has expanded considerably since I have been down here and eating three meals a day. I must go home and get back in the rhythm of my life style which is ever alert to preserve the precise figure demanded by the dietary lords who lay down the rules for an eighty-year-old gossoon [Irish for lad] on the way to eighty-one. Age, height, charm, whimsey all enter into this calculation in one way or another and who am I, who never doubted the authority of the Church, to go against any lesser breed. I know full well that for the past several years I have submitted to the seven pillars, to wit: Pronestyl, Panwarfarin, Isoderl, Dyrenium, Lanoxin, Lasix and Brandy, with a particular emphasis on the last as it seems to reach the very bullseye of what needs to be reached, especially when someone comes in like my doctor to share it with me. So you can see that it has a high place in the pharmacopeia of Ye Old Medicine Shoppe and rightly so. I simply can't wait to give you a spoonful when you come my way. I love to share with you all the good things that I enjoy: the Apostles Creed for instance, the Memorare, the Offertory prayers and the Jabberwocky. I have loads of other things too and I long for your presence to tell you about them.

For instance I was around here for a full week before I found anything fit to read outside of professional things. Then Charles brought down from upstairs a quadrant of books on Tolkien, including his biography. I have not been able to put it down and am just wild to get at the *Hobbit*, the *Lord of the Rings* and *Silmarillion*. I have heard and read about these for years and only now at my age am I going to enter into the Middle Earth and find what it is all about… No doubt you have already come in contact with them. Then how come you have been so silent? I can't imagine you not liking them, you who still dote on Alice and the Hunting of the Snark.

Next morning

…What I wanted to say immediately this morning is that it is very cold out as it has been every morning this week. No spear of snow or ice has returned to its component for two months, I am sure. The cold, together with the huge banks of snow, cause me to wilt and to think of the future in terms of igloos, walrus and fur pants. It is easy to imagine that we are returning to the ice age, not? Of course so long as the engine turns over in the morning and the heater is working there is no great need to worry. I am ready to go home, in fact I look eagerly to going home. I face the day with more equanimity in my own house or as the poets would say under my own rooftree, which is a word that must go back to the time of Middle Earth.

I got a peach of a letter from your sister Sarah. "Your neice, Sarah," she signs herself. Spelled that way it sounds like a Jabberwocky word, doesn't it? She is smart and I think I could draw her out if I took the trouble as lots of thoughts go on in that little noodle. She says herself that she thinks too much. Maybe I will take the trouble. She had just bought her first pair of jeans: "Whoever said that I have to follow along with societies anyway".... Who indeed! And a lovely Hallmark card came from Mary Kay with a rampant lion cradling behind his forefeet the most blissful little lamb with the one word Peace on the inside. She couldn't resist sending it to me—which tells me more about Mary Kay than a thousand words. So you have some unique sisters coming up behind you and we haven't even heard from Amy yet. That will be the day!!

The Retreat was the best ever. A Father Kaminski from Fall River, Mass. He runs the most unique parish in a dreadful section of Fall River—a brothel across the street and nobody out after dark on the streets. But it is an oasis of prayer and spiritual activity. He only gives four Retreats a year. He has gone back to Poland each year in the last ten, leads a pilgrimage to the Shrine of our Lady at Częstochowa each year and knows John Paul intimately. He told a good story on the latter when asked by a busybody reporter on what he thought would be his greatest problem in the Church. He answered: "Dandruff. I wonder will it show up against the white vestments?"....

Fr. Jerry Mahon and I took him up to catch his plane in Rochester and continued on to Worthington for the funeral next morning of the father of our seminarian who was home for Rome for the event. A wonderful liturgy with a crowded Church and in four inches of snow we took off for Caledonia where we arrived just in time to cut the birthday cake. There must be something about turning eighty that produced a very avalanche of Hallmarks from all directions....

The assembly of the Family Tree is becoming too formidable for my typing ability even with my new typewriter... I have all kinds of ideas but scarcely the will to carry them through, like Tolkien who took almost all his days to write *Silmarillion* and then his son had to finish it up for him. But his difficulty was that he was too prolix while mine is that I am too lazy... And that, my dear, is a whole heaven of difference!!!!!

I could close this letter anytime but I linger because I love you, I am full of prayers for you and the whole elective process of the Ursulines. Angela Merici the other day on her feast was very cooperative I thought as she said that she would arrange things properly in Brown County. So hold your whist as the Irish say and all things will turn out for the best… That card you bought at the Uncle Shop slayed me. Charles thought it was terrific. But you have a genius for choosing and selecting, e.g. The Ursulines of Brown County. And your parents and brothers and sisters. And the Lord. And your friends. And the lifestyle that is yours. And the Snark. God bless now and much much love....

Uncle Stanley

On Neighbors: Having Them, Being One, Living Near Them, Loving Them

"Yes, there is a 'new heaven' but there is also
a 'new earth' (Revelation 21:1). In this mutual indwelling
we no longer live just as ourselves, but in a larger force
field called the Body of Christ, webbed together
by the Holy Spirit."
— From The Center for Action and Contemplation
Richard Rohr Daily Meditation, July 9, 2021

"Last night I was wandering about in the neighborhood…"
—Uncle Stanley, letter 11

"I must eat now and get busy with a million things
after lunch, including twenty-minutes in a chair with my feet

up and my eyes shut and the world dashing by without a care.
In the meantime work hard, and play hard and love your
neighbor, which you are finding out is the hardest of all. Even
to think about her is difficult—at least when she is thinking
about you and wants to be noticed."
—Uncle Stanley, letter 32

"To love one's neighbor you have to have neighbors and only
the most dedicated anchoress can be content with God alone
for neighbor. A variety of neighbors is what the pie of community
calls for—something you can get your soul's teeth into."
—Uncle Stanley, letter 80

"Word and Sacrament are totally empty without love
for neighbor… They are drunk with God and the sobering
process lies in the area of love of neighbor… In the meantime,
love God, your neighbor, and me."
—Uncle Stanley, letter 149

Dear One,

I cannot listen to the impeachment proceedings, as vile as I find our President and his buddies. I cannot watch the tension at the border where neighbors, seeking safety and freedom are treated like animals and criminals. I cannot bear to witness how we are treating our creature-neighbors who languish helplessly at our greed and arrogance. I barely avoid imagining putting strychnine in the coffee of those I disdain.

I cower in the face of conflict. I freeze, clam up, turn the other cheek. Yet perhaps a good conflict is what it will take to get our sights set on true north again. Or perhaps we will come to realize that true north never really existed in our country or our world, despite our meager efforts. We were, after all, cast out of Eden for falling into the trap of thinking we knew what we were doing and what was best. What, after all, did we know?

But this reflection is about neighbors: having them, being one, loving each one.

Tom Junod, the inspiration for the film "A Beautiful Day in the Neighborhood," writes this month in *The Atlantic*: "What Would Mister Rogers Do?" What would he do in the face of so many challenges in our world: manifestos, polarization, white privilege? "Remembering him as a nice man is easier than thinking of him as a demanding one," Tom remarks. Perhaps he would demand kindness for all, even those we despise or feel better-than. Or perhaps he would demand a slower, slower, slowest pace, patiently waiting for each one to find that inner, wounded, wondering child? Or perhaps starting each day he would demand that we too cast aside our (my) well-practiced professionalism and put on the relaxing attire of presence? Or do something little rather than something big?

Two mantras: "you were a child once," and "look for the helpers" are essential to that demanding gospel that Mister Rogers espoused and lived. Yes, I, Ellen Marie Catherine Doyle, was a child once. Once there was space for mistakes. And time for play. And room for being dependent on someone else for the answer about what to do, how to do it. Once, long long ago. And if I really look for the helpers, they were (and are) there: Grandma's slow presence, Uncle Stanley's unconditional trust that I knew what I was doing with my life, Anne's friendship, Xavier's mentoring, Elaine's wisdom, Lucia's neighboring.

Lucia and I have found a lovely way to be neighbors: respecting each other's space and time, yet knocking and welcoming and sharing and checking-in and praying together. And now we have two new neighbors downstairs to welcome, to listen to, to share with, to be patient with.

But neighboring is bigger than just focusing on 510 Garfield Avenue. It includes the Black man I met today at the Post Office who greeted me with, "Happy Holidays." And happy holidays to you as well. Do you have family to share the holidays with? Yes, but this is the second year without our oldest son. Oh my. What happened? A drug overdose. Oh, I am so sorry. What a loss. Yet he is freed of his suffering. Yes, that's what we believe, what we know. Not many see it that way though… I wish I knew where he lives, this man who feels like a neighbor to me. Not that I would do anything, not even bring Christmas cookies or a card. But rather, it would give me hope to know on what street he is neighbor, on what street his suffering touches that of a handful of other neighbors who know suffering.

Uncle Stanley admonished me early on to be a neighbor, love my neighbor, sink my teeth into a variety of neighbors, the pie of community. He was never one to escape the world, even into God. His was a life lived among the people, rubbing elbows with the neighbors, on his street, in the pub, the library, the church, the cemetery, even in the literary pages of adventure and he invited me into the same. There is wisdom waiting for me as I enter into these weeks of staying home. Yet mine is not a life of solitude, not the anchoress's call, as tempting as that may be. I will call Roseanne, grieving from her brother's death and listen… before offering to set a date for lunch to celebrate her jubilee. Though not in my closest circle, Roseanne is a neighbor for sure. As is Mary, newly diagnosed with metastasized breast cancer. And the Sassons. And the soon-to-be-married bank manager Janina. And our elders at Mount Notre Dame. And eleven-year-old Ian at the Mayo Clinic. And Donald Trump. And Lucia. All children once, or still.

Peace to you, dear Neighbor,

Ellen

P.S. Write about a neighbor or two. One you loved. One who was like a stone in your shoe. Invite another neighbor in for tea and to hear you read what you wrote, out loud, with gusto (or tears)!

IN THE SEASON OF SUMMER

....

Letter II from Worthington, Minnesota

𝓜y dear Ellen,

Well, my love, I seem to have all the odd jobs done and now I can concentrate on more interesting things. It is a silly time to attempt anything really as it is 1:15 on a hot summer afternoon and one ought to be either taking a nap—that blessed gift that constantly escapes me—or be soaking in some lake or tub or been between a few breakers at Kitty Hawk. And maybe I will not persevere if something still more beguiling comes along. But that would have to be pretty enticing like the arrival of Phyllis Jordon who is a charmer about seventy with the strangest hallucinations. She might stop in with the intention of marrying me as I seem to call on her a lot. The other midnight I was riding with the police trying to figure out where her cries for help were coming from. She had no telephone, her house was barricaded, no lights appeared. On the impossible chance that she had a telephone installed we called the phone company where we drew a blank. Finally a third call and the police hung on to her until I could get there. She was home and had installed a telephone that afternoon. Shook! Me, I mean!

…Your mother wrote a letter before she left with the family for Kitty Hawk and was worried about her Tim and his budding romance. It sounds so familiar to us that I wonder if all mothers aren't suffering from the same thing—a simple fear of the unknown. People must go through all this with a growing, reaching-out family that are bound to go contrary to a mother's dreams. We will have to pray, don't you think, that she will not have to worry unduly. Then she told me about the prowler. That could terrify everybody, I suppose. But such a one would stand out in that community like Telestar.…

You have been a love to keep on writing even though I have not kept up. So many interesting things happen to you—at least in your mind—that you do have a lot to write about. When you get older the things in your mind do not seem to be worth stating on paper but actually that is due to a false humility, no doubt. Nobody, depending solely on happenings, can interest one for long. Just this morning I ran into a woman that insisted on squeezing out the very last drop of conversation that could be got out of trifle. By that time I was idling my patience. But on second thought I began to look at myself from the viewpoint of a boring old fool that must cause many a person to go gaga, tear their hair and send up cries of agony in the night. Actually one must love to enjoy what other people are saying. Especially people with nothing to say....

Last night I was wandering about in the neighborhood and trying to arouse an old lady who had been in the hospital to find out whether she would like to receive holy communion at home. Her son finally allowed me to approach close enough through a mass of barking dogs to permit me to hear that mama had been taken to Iowa to stay with a daughter.

But in the course of this attempt I saw through the windows of a hot night a couple talking to each other. I rapped at their door and they were overjoyed to see me and I was beginning to think I was something special when they let me know that before I had come they had been quarreling and that I was a life saver. They talked very frankly about their quarrel and how frequently they indulged in such and for the life of me I can't figure out yet whether quarreling was a legitimate means of communication to them. If they did not quarrel they didn't know what to say to each other. They always ended up friends. It lent spice to life.

So the paradox that presents itself is, or could be, that loving your neighbor is best evidenced by a good knock-down, drag-out fight. Which puts the holy or unholy confessors in a quandary. When people confess they are always quarreling and you give them hell maybe it is the worst kind of counseling. Maybe one should admonish them to see when they fought that they used legitimate, Marquis of Queensbury rules and did not ever hit below the belt or put strychnine in each other's coffee. It's hard to be a pastor sometimes!

I remember years ago in Rome our camerata was passing through a low-class neighborhood and a husband was beating the wife unmercifully. One of our lads, chivalrous, wearing white hat and riding a white horse and seeking "Involvement," dashed in and took the man in charge. But only for a moment as both husband and wife grabbed staves and took after the valiant young man and told him to mind his own business. I remember the wife was particularly vehement. Maybe because a man—a holy man, an ignorant Levite, dared to doubt her valor. She could well take care of herself and the whole episode probably robbed her and her husband of the joys of making up and they were never the same afterwards.

This sheet seems totally devoid of thought. Destroy it please….

You silly romantic, you reading *The Anchorhold*. I remember giving copies of that book away to friends eons ago. I had forgotten about Enid Dennis and her tale but a whole wide picture came to mind when you mentioned the book….

Yes, do not worry about what you are. Just be yourself. You are plenty, plenty. Don't try to imitate anybody. It is precisely you and not another that so delights me, I know. Not your resemblance to Nazimova, Helen of Troy or the Witch of Endor. Or any Hale or Quinn or Doyle, etc. And God bless you, my dear.

Affectionately,

Uncle Stanley

P.S. I may go off to Long Island this next week. To sun my carcass and lick my wounds. I have several of the latter. JSH

Letter 32

My dear Ellen Doyle,

I do not expect to fill this sheet but it is a legal-size piece of paper that leaps easily into my typewriter just begging for words, punctuation and diacritical marks. Since I leap too and if left undisturbed may by chance fill the whole damn thing it is just as well to have a solid base of ground up wood under the print to make it legible even though the burden of thought may be too much for the frail vessels that must carry it. I have a picture in my portfolio of Things Past of the northern and southern ends of a small donkey worrying his way up a steep hill near Frascati with a great fat Capuchin astride in full regalia. Whenever I want to get a homely image of a B.C.U., frail in stature like Sandy, mighty in purpose like Bert, carrying about great headsful of brains I get out my little picture and marvel at the ways of the Lord. The point I am actually trying to make is this: I have just read your letter (before supper). It has been on my desk all day and only then was I able to sit comfortably back and read it with the solemn pleasure it deserved.

After supper I had to say Mass and now I am just in after giving a short homily on the weariness that must have possessed Christ every time he locked horn with the stuffed shirts of his time, the Pharisees. So many of these Lenten gospels are concerned with this confrontation that one wonders if the Church isn't very pointedly talking to all of us. In spite of myself I have been scraping over my conscience with no fine comb (not needed) and am getting scared as hell. It seems to me that the spitting image of John Q. Pharisee is John Stanley Hale. I strain at gnats and swallow camels; I am a whited sepulcher (somewhat dirtied from the vicissitudes of life). I am full of dead men's bones. (If they were alive I certainly would feel more like flying to Rome.) The obtuseness of the breed is simply inhuman. One ought to be able to tumble to the truth that confronts them. Is it human respect, is it that diabolical solidarity of men who would rather go down to hell together than break away and fly a lonely course to heaven? And why should the path to heaven be so lonely? Absent thee from Roberta for a while and riddle me this. And do expatiate on community. How many does it take to make a community? Four that fill a car and one left out to grieve?...

Next afternoon-and the snow coming down gently but persistently, inch by inch, flake by flake until it fills the whole landscape, the whole of my spring-oriented mind, the whole gorge that does not lie in any mountainous district but right between your gullet and your spleen. Here it is apt to explode into a landslide that will cover everything to a depth of forty feet, especially all those romantics that happily exclaim, "Oh, the snow, the snow, the beautiful snow." So run to your houses, pick up the shovels, turn out the tractor, the blower, the snowmobiles and get to work my hearties. Who told you that spring was just around the corner?...

FRIDAY Morning
This is getting long enough to send.

I don't know whether to be happy for Roberta over her decision or sorry for the nieces who will not be able to share their lives with her. Just think of all the people in this one area of human activity who will never have known her presence or appreciated her worth. Of course there will be a whole new group that will now be affected by her charm, her mind, her gifts. They are the lucky ones. But she must walk to God by her own road and we can only pray that it is a straight road, and happy and paved with gold. What a pity that she will walk this road and so many thousands will never know that they should have looked and doffed their hats and waved their banners because a queen was passing by, God bless her.

Where are you going to get the Daiquiris to celebrate Dolores and Carol's birthdays this month? You will have to find a supplier now that your father is changing his accent. He may be going in for mint juleps and that is a long, long way from rum, Romanism and Ursulanism. After all the spirit of Ursulanism is in POVERTY. That's what I read and that's what I believe. Community of course but Holy Poverty. What you have given up I don't know yet but you are right when it isn't wealth, things, but everything, as Carol says, but Trust. That takes a lot of doing…

I must eat now and get busy with a million things after lunch, including twenty-minutes in a chair with my feet up and my eyes shut and the world dashing by without a care. In the meantime work hard, and play hard and love your neighbor, which you are finding out is the hardest of all. Even to think about her is difficult—at least when she is thinking about you and wants to be noticed.

God bless.

My love to the girls,

Uncle Stanley

P.S. Tom Quinn called up to say that he had put your grandmother in the hospital with pneumonia. He thought she would be all right. I shall try to see her Monday. A line to her would be Madelia Municipal Hospital. JSH

....

Letter 80, with Christmas Card

My dear Ellen dear,

Your grandmother, like John the Baptist, goes before you into Carolina. She left today. I talked to her last night and I was lucky I did because only yesterday did I dump or have dumped all my Christmas cards into the mail chute and she would have gone off without a word had I not called. She is in fine fettle and is looking forward to the day when you arrive and make her happiness complete. So am I….

IN THE SEASON OF SUMMER

This day that came out of fifteen degrees of cold has me shivering... I haven't had my nose out since Sunday when it was all but bitten off by the frost—it, the cold, simply stops my breathing. I am to go to a Children's Christmas party tonight and I don't know whether I can make it or not even though a family will pick me up in a warm car and bring me home again. You can see why I am looking out the window at the sky so often. I am looking to see a late migratory bird headed South hoping to catch a ride on his wing. Were it headed for Arizona, and you can see I get very little time to inquire, I would leap aboard, I think. I am still not sure whether I should venture.... In the meantime I have had ample time to work on a few hundred Christmas cards and I am getting close to the end of the letters. I still have the seventy-five or so locals cards to get out but I don't send any in the parish unless I receive one. It has been a labor of love and I have attempted to cheer up everybody and arouse them to shout RAH, Rah, Rah to God. After all, our own method of praise, that has come out of mouths of a whole new species of people that we call cheerleaders, should be a dandy addition to the Holy, Holy, Holy of the Angels. As for the cards that come in some have only a name, a conscience bit with a stamp on it. Others show a degree of enthusiasm for a moment and then like the seed that fell on stony ground, dry up. Some contain one sentence urging me to write a long letter—"I just love to get your letters"—but now and again a long, long letter like one I received from a lady in Charles City, Iowa of nine pages. Delightful! And every time she gets off a bit of humor it is followed by HO!HO!HO!HO! four times. She is a dear soul and lived in the parish about five years and has been gone about eight. Some contain money and they burn my soul and I am moved to share it with you if you can find the enclosed. You and Anne can blow it enroute on Daiquiris or whatsoever....

I have been praying much for you as I think you are upset. Calm down dear one and let Him fix it up on YOUR knees. It appears to me that if your age group and think-alikes are content with the status quo you can sway others to that same status quo. Instead, I am convinced that the community is everything and any fragmentation whatsoever simply opens the door to emptiness. To love one's neighbor you have to have neighbors and only the most dedicated anchoress can be content with God alone for neighbor. A variety of neighbors is what the pie of community calls for—something you can get your soul's teeth into.

But this is Christmas and I must exude a little Christmas spirit. I hope you have a joyful, happy day and that you will get yourself rested for the long grind until spring. Spread your largess far and broad for your gifts are many. Love greatly for you are loved greatly. Why even I love you more and more each day!

God bless you

Uncle Stanley

....

Letter 149

St. Patrick's Day
My dear Ellen,

Irish blood is boiling today, arousing old loyalties, old animosities against the Sassenach, old love for the Faith. Your mother bestirred herself early this morning and got on the phone to declare her patriotism. I was delighted to hear her because when they called last time on the eve of your Father's trip to Italy, I was asleep and trying to get rid of a monumental cold that locked me in for three weeks. Thank God I have come through that with all its attendant medication and reactions to medication. I am a new man and have been pounding the life out of this machine to make up for lost time. Even now I am just back from a good, brisk walk down to the recreational center where they are putting up a new billiard room and where the people were bowling on the green. I watched for some time while I generated enough energy to walk back. Now we await Betty Cashman to come in and celebrate the day with us and stay to dinner while I read the many letters that came in while I was gone. St. Patrick instigated all of them, bless him. I am sure that down in Cincinnati his name is never mentioned but there ought to be a few of your pals stemming from the old Sod to gather together and lift one in his honor and the honor of the race. There is no convent in the world that does not enclose a stray daughter of Erin. That is what we used to say in Rome. I remember one coming down the steps of the Cancelleria one day as I was going up. She recognized me and opened her mouth in surprise so wide that her teeth fell out and I caught them in my hand. What a blessed day that was for the Little Sisters of the Poor!…

…As a meditation out here I go back to the notes of my last retreat which I attended just before I came. This morning was a plea of what kind of open, loving, sensitive pastor a priest should be. Essential priority to love my neighbor-as I have loved you. Love of God is full of illusions: how do you love God whom you cannot see.… Word and Sacrament totally empty without love for neighbor.

How do I handle the man I detest—except through Jesus? Qualities of service: to wish the best for every person—the shalom of Christ. To judge a person is to kill him, to cut one down by word or look. How to unleash the love in our hearts—everybody is dying to be loved and to love. To the American priest, Church, faith, celibacy remain negative—they call us Father. Act like a father. Be a warm, affectionate man. Don't deny your humanity—love your people, weep for them. Of course you will get hurt. Become involved, communicate your uniqueness. The people want a wonderful wholesome man. Pray to be a lover, a man who cares…

I feel like starting all over again. Why can't a man grasp this at the beginning of his life instead of at the end? Same with a Sister of course and you are in the very thick of the fray… They are drunk with God and the sobering process lies in the area of love of neighbor… Holiness is an abrasive process as you are finding out…

I would ask you, did you ever cash that $25.00 check I sent you for Christmas? No matter but I wonder that my check-book doesn't balance—I'm a lousy balancer—to the tune of $25.00 and I am not home to check my checks. I enclose another twenty for Easter. I hope to talk to you over the phone when I get back in my own house. In the meantime, love God, your neighbor, and me.

So much love…

Uncle Stanley

On Cecilia

"I hope you had a happy time at Ceil's Halloween party. How neat of her to think it up. 'We have been working too hard, all of us, let's do some crazy things: You come as a skeleton, you a pirate, you a shepherd and you as Jesse James. We will serve tea, Hudepohl, crackers and cheese. We will give each person a chance to do her thing, the crazier the better.' That sort of thing, eh! How human, how communitarian…!"
—Uncle Stanley, letter 142

"PS. I think I must have to write to Ceil too to let her know that I help her to hold up her arms like Moses was held up as the battle raged."
—Uncle Stanley, letter 155

*D*ear One,

J. Stanley Hale died August 26, 1985, in Worthington, Minnesota. The following letter, dated August 6, 1985, twenty days before he died, may have been the last one Uncle Stanley wrote to anyone. It was sent to Sr Cecilia (aka Ceil) Huber who had just moved from St. Martin, Ohio, to St. Mary's, Alaska, for a new ministry after serving as our Ursuline Congregational Minister for six years. She gave me all of his letters to her before she died in 2017.

My dear Sister Cecilia,

My history of the parish is all done and the very first letter I am going to write is to that self-flagellating nun who chooses to dash off to one of the dropping-off places of the world where she can atone for all her sins of commission and omission after being in the seat of the Almighty. She will now live in an igloo, eat raw fish, blubber and whatever the frozen sea has to offer. She will be as happy as all get out. I know, for her disposition is such that she will enjoy all others in exactly the same degree of longitude, if there is any longitude left in that isolated community. But I would like to see you in your cariboo skin and fur pants. My picture of your benighted land comes from a book I read years and years ago called Kabloona. It was a book about a French newsman who chose to live among the eskimos all one winter. The picture that comes to mind was that of two eskimos and himself overcome in a foray by a violent snow storm. They found shelter in an empty igloo built for that very purpose where there were buried in the walls two dead frozen seals. They spread their blankets on raised ice seats and the two eskimos attacked the seals with their teeth. They ate voraciously the raw food, spitting bones all over the floor and upsetting the stomach of the poor newsman by their gastronomical exploits. So, Sister dear, should you allow yourself to become more primitive at least use a knife, fork and spoon. And don't ruin the carpet with fish bones.

I talked to Ellen on Saturday… and Anne and Carol and Ellen are off to Wrightsville Beach today. They will have wonderful time and I would like to be with them. But I am lucky to get out the door these days. Today it is too hot and humid so I shelter myself behind the air-conditioner. I must say I am feeling quite well today as you may note from the tone of this letter. I hope that it is the beginning of getting my strength back. My vision has been affected by a growing cataract that seems to have caught speed from all the radiation. No matter so long as I can type and you can correct the mistakes I make.

God bless you dearly and a BIG Welcome to the Mission. I know you do what I do—1ive by the line in the post-Our Father-prayer at Mass: "Protect us from all anxiety as we wait in joyful hope for the coming of our Savior, Jesus Christ...."

Much love,

Uncle Stanley

Cecilia taught with me at Ursuline Academy and was adopted as one of "the nieces" when Uncle Stanley came to know her during his visits to Cincinnati. They wrote to each other periodically and were soulmates, always playfully sharing their love with the wider community. To know that his last letter was to her was a comfort. I wait in joyful hope to have a grand reunion with both of them!

Hoping that you too are living in joyful hope!

A friend of friends,

Ellen

P.S. Draw a diagram of your friends and your friend's friends and your friend's friend's friends. Use stickers if you have any to celebrate all the connections!

....

Letter 142

All Souls Day

*M*y dearest Ellen,

Your letter just came in the door. I was dawdling over a cup of coffee as I had no lunch because breakfast was late on account of my three Masses which were late because I had to go to the Clinic for my monthly blood tests. I was reading in my red book in which I had written so many things in my youth, (many sound absurd now but they indicate youthful enthusiasms).

    Now that we have a mood established, we can carry on… I hope you had a happy time at Ceil's Halloween party. How neat of her to think it up. "We have been working too hard, all of us, let's do some crazy things: You come as a skeleton, you a pirate, you a shepherd and you as Jesse James. We will serve tea, Hudepohl, crackers and cheese. We will give each person a chance to do her thing, the crazier the better." That sort of thing, eh! How human, how communitarian!…

Saturday

…All Saints Eve while waiting for the tricks and treats to start I picked up Margaret of Cortona again by Mauriac and I have scarcely been able to put it down. Talk about instant and total giving. She became so crazed with love of the Lord that everybody thought her crazy. And I suppose she was. Every Saint must be if we talk about deviation from the normal. But I do think more examples of holiness should be put before people rather than methods of prayer or what is now known as spiritual reading. Teresa [of Avila] of course is the vade mecum [that is, a handbook or guide that is kept constantly at hand for consultation] for all who dare the religious life.

You know it just came over me how very ridiculous I am in offering advice or even commentary on the religious life to such as you. I really know nothing about it. I would never in a thousand year accepted a chaplaincy of a nunnery. I would run for my life (no doubt with the devil jogging along with me) as I never felt adequate enough to guide souls to holiness. I sympathize with Teresa when she had to put up with so many mediocrities. As I said before I have only one thing to offer and that is the talent of the heart. I do and I can love and identify with you and all the others. But love isn't enough sometimes. Such also demands horse sense....

I will redouble my prayers for you as I can see you do suffer at times. You need a visit at my house! Luckily you can look forward to the break at Thanks Day when the lovers will be gathering around. But that is three weeks off so I thought I would help out by getting this to you statim (that is immediately, in Latin). I love you dearly as you know. I would like to be able to supply you with other ingredients that would help you in your loving task. But I am just your uncle after all and no angel of the apocalypse.

All yours,

Uncle Stanley

....

Letter 155

Monday morning
*D*ear Ellen, Ellen,

Godfrey Dieckmann of St. John's University, told Sr. Mary Willette in class last week that the Lord said Martha, Martha is a sign of her specialness and endearment so since I have often done the same I thought I would start this letter with Ellen, Ellen, for of all the specially dear people on land or sea to me you are the mostest. And being the mostest I am beginning to think that if I continue to feel as I do these past weeks I would venture a trip to Cincy to see you and the special family who also hold you dear....

Your last note before departure I just reread and rediscover that this period of transition from one state of activity to another finds your gut lagging behind your head. For a spiritual person in love with God that is an ordinary happening, is it not? He is always way ahead of us, waiting for us to catch up. I often thought this business of waiting on the Lord is just the opposite; he is the one who is waiting. It is so hard for us to give up routine, the rhythm of our existence and shifting gears can be a very painful process. But when one accepts a vocation at his hands, make a total gift of oneself, shout brave words over the sonar system of our mutual communication lines, we simply have to let him call the terms. We simply can't have anything to say any more after we say, "I do" in the first place. It would be grand if we could just catch a glimpse through the fog, but—

"Those shaken mists a space unsettle,
then round the half-glimpsed turrets, slowly wash again....

Halts by me that footfall;
Is my gloom, after all,
Shade of His hand outstretched caressingly?"
—From the "Hound of Heaven" by Francis Thompson

Maybe it is just the process of change, what you have to go through to bring about the change that bothers you more than anything else. And then there is the juggling of your friends; the necessity to enfold more publicly and the few lest intimately that is causing distress. But surely you must realize that you have been growing and growing so that you were all but ready to burst out of the status quo into something more commensurate with your powers. All God's gifts must be used (sounds as if I were talking myself into a martini) and in your case they could not be exercised in doing just what you have been doing. So line up your gut with your head and heart and carry on...

...When my mind leaps to the Ohio I can only think of you- even if you have leapt to the ocean. I envy you a small bit lying on a beach surrounded by loved ones. I hope all goes well there and that you are very happy to be with them all. Extend my love to them and bring home a tan that is discussable and arouses envy. There is no need to go to all that work unless you can carry it like a flag!

God love you dearly and all present. I love you very much and thank God for you day-by-day. (I could make a song of it like a lyric from *Godspell*.)

Uncle Stanley

PS. I think I must have to write to Ceil too to let her know that I help her to hold up her arms like Moses was held up as the battle raged.

Teaching & Mentoring

On Chemistry Tests and Retorts

"Only through the community will you become holy—only through your relationship with people—and not through the retorts and Bunsen burners that are your special portion of the institution. I never do expect you to write a book someday entitled: "I found God among the Bunsen burners"—a little heat there maybe, a little light, but not the Light of Lights, not the Heat of Heats—unless of course you use all your daily clutter and that special way that gives honor and glory to God."
—Uncle Stanley, letter 60

"No matter how many retorts or even torts get between you and your pupils it is you the Sister, the dedicated one, the loving sister, the understanding friend, that will make their lives. Wherever you are placed, whatever you are called on to do by the voice that ultimately summons, the reason for your calling lies in the love and salvation of your pupils...."
—Uncle Stanley, letter 60

Dear One,

I attended the ninetieth birthday of the mother of two former students of mine on Saturday. I taught them both chemistry in the 1970s. One loved chemistry and became a pediatrician. One struggled with chemistry and is a physical therapist. They are both married with children in their twenties. One remembered the test I prepared for the periodic chart: a blank chart with descriptors of the qualities of "fake" elements. The puzzle captivated her and she remembers it almost fifty years later. It so motivated her that she said she went off to Boston College and then medical school with the confidence that she would have what she needed. The other remembered me sitting with her one-on-one and patiently explaining the complex meanings of a "mole." Her grown son listened as she remembered that high school experience and proclaimed that he loves moles, as his mother looked at me warmly.

Having both girls reach out to me several years ago as their father was dying and now as their mother is celebrating her milestone birthday is a precious gift. A confirmation that Uncle Stanley's almost obsession with getting me out of the lab and into more spiritual or pastoral ministry was unfounded. God works through us wherever we are and weaves the secular and the sacred together in such lovely designs that we need not worry! My seven years teaching chemistry equipped me to navigate a world where science is questioned, where creation-centered theology deepens our care for our earth and where students who loved chemistry and students what hated chemistry can celebrate learning!

Farewell, my friend,

Ellen

P.S. Write about one subject you had in high school that you loved (or hated) and how that teacher shaped the person you became.

....

Letter 60 from Worthington, Minnesota

My dear girl,

It is 7:00 PM. I just finished the dishes—a pedestrian meal of ham steak, fried potatoes, fresh tomatoes (the seeds of these have entered my bloodstream so many have I eaten) plus some applesauce I made Tuesday and a few cookies (given to me by my good friends among the cookie-makers). Not at all imaginative—but I used up my imagination today on a spaghetti sauce concoction consisting of golden fried onions and green peppers, ground round steak, stewed tomatoes, plus tomato paste, chili powder, ground cumin, bay leaves, oregano, wine, mushrooms etc. I put it away in the deep freeze until you appear at Easter. In very truth, I am practicing the most gourmet absurdities so that when you come, we will eat, drink and be merry—after we pray, fast and abstain during Lent. It seems so long: the way to Easter. And this cheerful outlook on life which takes for granted that we will live forever gives me qualms. But I console myself that if I cannot entertain Ellen D(ear) in Worthington I can meet her in heaven with a rousing choir singing: "Yahweh called me before I was born!" just to welcome you and make you feel at home....

Your letter yesterday was perfect. I knew you would be disturbed about the opening of school and meeting a new class and I intended to get a letter to you to steady your hand. But I was writing letters to everybody else and didn't quite get to it. Now that you have already plowed deep in the serried furrows of your class, you do not need a word of encouragement so much as congratulations that you are entering into it in the spirit of your community at Blue Ash.

[I bet you are wondering what "serried furrows" means! Maybe this context will help: "May he whose waist is girded keep you safe. Yea, he whose serried furrows brightly shine." From *Vasavadatta, A Sanskrit Romance*.]

You are so right that the community must be everything and the institution secondary. Only through the community will you become holy—only through your relationship with people—and not through the retorts and Bunsen burners that are your special portion of the institution. I never do expect you to write a book someday entitled: "I found God among the Bunsen burners"—a little heat there maybe, a little light, but not the Light of Lights, not the Heat of Heats—unless of course you use all your daily clutter and that special way that gives honor and glory to God. And, of course, this is what you'll have to do, as the day is so demanding that you tumble into bed exhausted, without any quiet time for "talk." So get in the habit of building all activity, all relationships, around Him so that if you can't meet Him head-on, as it were, and few can or have the time, you can catch him on the fly. This is what Francis Thompson meant I think when he used the phrase: "Clinging to heaven by the hems." But maybe he meant something far less. Love finds a way to penetrate all obstacles, like a drop of oil on a shiny stone floor. If the will is there the method will take care of itself. This is an old saw indeed. Excuse it…!

You have driven your piton on the perpendicular face of the great massif and the next one will be driven in far above it. If so away you go, bright angel, on the great adventure. Don't get too far away that you can't talk to me. Or better yet take me with you. I will do the cooking….

God love you very much. I do—

Uncle Stanley

....

Letter 71

Monday afternoon
My dear Ellen,

About the time I talked to you last night the weather, which had been icky all day, suddenly took on a serious whine. This morning when I woke up the spring blizzard was on with schools closed and highways shut down… It stretched all the way across the state and from top to bottom-which is so very unusual as weather in one section of this huge state is not weather in another. So I am frozen to my desk—or let us say to the seat of my pants as this is the very first effort I have made all day. The storm is abating and I could go to the hospital to see my special patients there whom I visit every day as they are terminal and need consolation.

But I just stuck my nose out the door and it said stay home so I am staying....

I am in a dither over what has happened in Vietnam—the poor, poor people, the ravaged, unhappy, wounded, people who see their whole world come tumbling down with no place to go. And the diplomats and the media looking on as if a herd of cattle had just fallen into a chasm. A woeful world and it becomes more and more woeful.

Which reminds me that concern for those who agonize far away should awaken me to the hearts that grieve nearer home. I have several coming in just now and this week I listened to a tale that flabbergasted me but when it was told and lying there on the floor the healing process set in and a confession was heard and one felt the glow of the eternal light....

What creatures we are—even we who have been called and chosen from our mother's womb to do something special! It has come home to me during these days of Lent that we have been very reluctant indeed to live up to the challenge of this supernatural selection (I call it). Ever since I tried to meditate on the gospel for the Tuesday of the fourth week of Lent (John 5: 1-3, 5-16) I have been bugged. Heretofore I always thought it a foreign bit in the Gospel of John and wondered why it was ever selected to read in the Mass. This thirty-eight-year-old invalid always seemed to me a lazy, surly bastard who didn't deserve his sudden good health. The Lord didn't even demand faith from him and later on when he ran into him in the temple didn't even thank him but dashed back to kow-tow to the powers that it was Jesus who cured him. No wonder Our Lord threatened him: "Go and sin no more or something worse will befall you." For years I couldn't make anything of the incident. And then one fine day it dawned on me that this stinker was the spitting image of John Stanley Hale.

For years, for far more than thirty-eight years the Lord would stir the waters of grace at a Retreat, when I read something that particularly appealed, when I ran into simple goodness, I would make a great stir and try to plunge into the pool of God's love, but I always got sidetracked before I could make it. I would blame somebody else-nobody really cared, somebody was always interfering, so I went back to the mat of mediocrity and was content with my malaise. But the Hound had been pursuing all the time and finally came along and without Aye, Yes or No, blasted me out of there and told me to get moving. He healed me with one stroke-a beautiful heart attack—which is no way to heal a man but it is often God's way and He often uses such contrivances as an automobile accident, a brain tumor, MS, or cancer or some such lovely medicine that He keeps in the apothecary shop of Heaven. Then one looks back and shakes one's head! How is it possible for God's love to put up with such inertia for so many years without acting sooner since He is going to act later? Of course I shudder at the thought of his not acting at all. Imagine how ashamed one would be to slide down the banister into the halls of death with nothing to show but a few feeble attempts to reach the pool!

That is why we cannot rest… Everybody is hungry, looking for a morsel to eat, a good word, a firm conviction, a loving heart, an image of Jesus. No matter how many retorts or even torts get between you and your pupils it is you the Sister, the dedicated one, the loving sister, the understanding friend, that will make their lives. Wherever you are placed, whatever you are called on to do by the voice that ultimately summons, the reason for your calling lies in the love and salvation of your pupils.…

Easter Monday
The cold still persists, snow flurries and damp and nasty. All week long, the week of the twin blizzards, it has been so and Easter morning dawned just nine above zero… In the afternoon I was called out to pray for Glenis Kellen who has been dying in the hospital since I was there. All her girls were home and we had an excellent prayer service around her bed. She died during the night. They wanted me to take charge of the funeral but I will be taking off that day early. Moreover it is an agreement that I

would attend the funerals, concelebrate when desired but not offer Mass or preach. She died a saint I am sure and has gone to heaven to meet the Lord coming from the tomb. Afterwards a nurse asked me to stop in at a room where a Lutheran family asked me to pray. Papa was dying, mother had been married to him for sixty years, and a great number of people were in the room. I did the same thing there and they were all in tears and so very very grateful. ECUMENISM!

God bless, now. I love you.

I would love to see you.

Uncle Stanley

On Tightrope Walking and Other Balancing Tricks

"The people I love the best
jump into work head first
without dallying in the shallows
and swim off with sure strokes almost out of sight."
—From "To Be of Use" by Marge Piercy

"My dear girl, I somehow get the impression from the blue stationery this morning that you have one foot in a bucket of syrup."
—Uncle Stanley, letter 19

*D*ear One,

I do wonder what I said in my letters to Uncle Stanley that first year in the convent that led to his alert about the importance of rest, the dangers of exhaustion. It seems that I have learned a bit of balance in my life by now, though I am still no tight-rope walker. And I still count on both a safety net and the gear to save me from myself.

My disciplined commitment to keep the Sabbath with focused attention since 1998 (with no work, email, social media, shopping, laundry, bill-paying, all to make room for rest, reading, being in community, prayer) has saved my life more than once. And my 2016 clarity around letting my "yes" mean "yes" and my "no" mean "no" to prospective work has deepened my commitment to make time for discernment in the face of any new ministry project and been a life-changing grace. But even so, those close to me who can read my soul still caution me to get some rest when they see my tallow skin color or hear the flatness in my voice.

So many of my twenty-three nieces and nephews, most now at the age I was when Uncle Stanley wrote to me, also lead frenetic lives. They work too hard, never unplug from their devices, and rarely stop for rest. In many ways our present age is one where we cannot see much farther than the week ahead and what we can see seems so dire and discouraging that working ourselves to death or being constantly distracted seems an easier path than dealing with the challenges of the world....

But children are born, reconciliation is hard won, and crises are overcome. There is hope! Getting the rest I need to celebrate that good news, to do the work that is mine to do, and to be faithful in fighting for justice and peace in our world remains a priority.

My grandmother used to always end her letters to me with "Don't work too hard, honey!" I wish for you such a wise grandmother.

My love, as ever,

Ellen

P.S. Any balancing tricks in your stockpile? How good are you at balancing in the midst of your busy life?

IN THE SEASON OF SUMMER

....

Letter 19 from Worthington, Minnesota

Thursday morning
My dear girl,

I somehow get the impression from the blue stationery this morning that you have one foot in a bucket of syrup. Not from anything you said but from subjects touched upon-like Thanksgiving with tears, Sandy and her back, and your inordinate exhaustion. This latter I can appreciate-the pace you go, I have been wondering how you have been able to bear the burden of your go-go personality. But I note compensations—like new people who affect you like pennies from heaven. Your all-out delight in your friends is a thing to see and to glory in and to thank God for. It stretches the heart until it becomes flexible enough to embrace the world. And it lays it open to suffering-like what we miss on holidays. Like, maybe, my phone call that I promised. It would not be a thing that would make or break a day but added to a stack of other inconsequentials and maybe consequentials it could, God help us, precipitate a cry if not a crisis.

 I myself felt bad about it when, half-way to Marshall to dine with Mary Pat at 3:30 in the afternoon I thought of what I had failed to do at 10:00 AM. But right after the most wonderful Mass with trumpets and patriotic hymns and processions and prayers and all the children and the fruits of the earth and packed church, I dashed off to visit with a lady, mother of four, who was to go into the hospital that afternoon for her second cancer operation. I stayed and talked with the family for some considerable time and then went to the hospital to check. I was really disturbed. She and her husband are both converts of mine. They are good faithful plodders in the work-a-day world and she helps in our cafeteria. Nothing handsome except her enormous love for everybody. I heard about it when I got back from Minneapolis the evening before. (Incidentally, she is doing well but her parents, brother, and a sister also went that road.) Even so let us say that my promise fell thru a hole in my memory. More damn things are escaping that way. It must be my age....

The exuberance of Snoopy moved me to put my pen to paper immediately. I am not altogether sure that there is more joy in convents over the reception of one piece of first-class mail than on the rejection of ninety-nine pieces of second-class mail. Still I am always willing to take a chance with the hope that joy will be unconfined.

So God bless you, get enough sleep, love your enemies, (I haven't heard about those yet.) be good to Sandy and read Isaiah the prophet.

Love,

Uncle Stanley

On Yes and No and I Don't Know

"Let your 'Yes' mean 'Yes' and your 'No' mean 'No'."
—Matthew 5:37

"You can't say 'No' to people and everything
is embraced by your big heart."
—Uncle Stanley, letter 90

"I am not surprised that they are courting their finger on you for administration. You have so many talents and could be anything you choose to be. But then there is your preference and what you would be best at. I can see how you are inclined to move slowly in this. But this is just another thing for the Lord to decide."
—Uncle Stanley, letter 104

> "You have got your fingers in too many pies, on too many wrists taking too many pulse-beats, sharing too many griefs."
> —Uncle Stanley, letter 150

*D*earest One,

Almost five years ago now, I made a retreat that sprang from the wise words of Matthew: "Let your Yes mean Yes and your No mean No." That verse was in the gospel the day I left for retreat. That retreat came after a six-month period of back-to-back work travel that came about because I had said "yes" when I should have said "no" too often, too carelessly, too driven by the false sense of my indispensability. There were also six more months of the same intensity on my calendar after the retreat.

Earlier, once I had woken up to what I had done to myself and why, I protected thirteen weeks from all travel so as to have a real break to re-group, re-center, and rest. When that break came, I grew into a deeper understanding of my compulsion to say "yes," my inclination to question if anyone could do whatever it was as well as I could, and my worries about having enough to do. And my life-balance shifted from the "doing" end of life's continuum toward "being." Re-claiming my response to my Dad's list of possible things-to-do that he presented me when I visited the family on the North Carolina coast for vacation was a big help! "Dad," I said, "what I most want to do is 1) go-to-the-beach, 2) read, 3) sleep, 4) eat and 5) do nothing!" After a few years of that he added these five favorite things to his list!

Now my mantra in the face of a "yes" or a "no" is "I don't know." I do not quickly say "yes," but rather claim some time for putting the possibility in perspective, giving time for watching, waiting, wondering, before making a decision. Nor do I quickly say "no" but rather ask first if this is really mine to do? Am I being called to this? Or not?

Sitting in the posture of not-knowing has made all the difference. My breathing is softer. My neck is more resilient. My sleep is deeper. My sense is that I am much more aligned with God's purpose for me in this world.

And there is time for fun, for creativity, for prayer, for time with those I love, for "doing nothing." Though, if truth be told, I still respond to my friend and colleague Tim Gavin when he asks for what he can pray for me: "Balance, Tim. Yes, please still pray for Balance."

I do not know what your own balance is like: in your life, in your work and outside of work. But I wonder. And I hope you do too!

Blessings to you, for balance in your work and in your play, in your "yeses" and in your "nos,"

Ellen

P.S. Put the words "I don't know…" on a piece of paper and let your pen take it from there! Notice how you feel as the words emerge… Or maybe list ten "yeses" from the last week and what brought you to each "yes."

....

Letter 90

Dear Ellen dear,

I just finished my sewing a button on my favorite jacket and a belt band on a brand-new rabbi I bought. One side was missing. I cut off an old one and supplied it rather than send it back to be finished. Both jobs were pretty awful when I consider your expertise as displayed in that lovely white dress your mother had on last Saturday night as I met them all in Windom on Saturday night for dinner. She wore it proudly, to the manner born and looked lovely with her big Italian glasses and solemn demeanor....

Next day
Do you know I am going to be very considerate and not demand many letters from you this year although they are rich food for my soul and

almost necessary for my ego-to be assured you love me and are willing to take pains. But I can see that you are being crowded with things to do and you must go to bed exhausted every night. You can't say "No" to people and everything is embraced by your big heart. To expect you at the end of one of your busy days to sit down and pour yourself out in a letter would be too, too selfish. But I so think you could ring me up oftener on reverse and it wouldn't take long... For phone calls I have unlimited funds. For your phone calls I have unlimited time. To receive such tokens of your love I have a big heart. So ring away! To respond I have unlimited time and will continue to write copiously. Do not get guilt feelings when you receive one-just accept it as your due... It is in the morning when I give myself to prayer that the heart opens up and also the day and I am moved to write to Ellen. And as the Lord, as you say, sends his consolations and assurances so as to keep us centered so we never lose heart, I too am moved to put out flags of verbiage and bunting of love to cheer you as you go, to make your feet happy, your mind supple and your heart sing. Or else what is an uncle for?

I love Phyllis' dreams that all took off to walk to my house. Wouldn't that be something to see you all walk in? She, bless her, could take over the cooking. I would be a congenial host only-with no work to do of any kind. Try to translate such dreams into reality... I can see that you are starting off with the front line in your palm for the year. Regina, Phyllis and you could set a plan for holiness that could change the face of the earth. With Gráinne and Catie to back you could set the tempo for the house. Please be ready to report on this when you call next time.

Whenever you mention Mary Inkrot's name in a letter which has been often I react with a burst of tenderness for the dear child. I pray that she clings to her angel and keeps on listening. She too will help to change the face of the earth.

This is gradually becoming a fetish with me. I am so conscious of my life's lack of proper motivation and the consequent building up of my own image instead of Christ's that I don't want others to make the same mistake and waste a whole life on idols. When one thinks of a young person drunk with God and filled up with Christ- what he or she could do to further His kingdom—it makes one frantic to see it come about. To live Christ—when St. Paul thinks about this he almost goes nuts and jumps out of Asia and all the way into Europe but just look what he did! It's women's work, nowadays, otherwise why this freedom to experiment, to try. Women's Lib certainly must be in truth the liberty to missionize, to preach the Gospel....

Ah, well I must close as it is time to go to the parade. I love you very much....

God bless

Uncle Stanley

....

Letter 104

Assumption 3:00 PM
My dearest girl,

It is a beautiful letter. It came Saturday when so many good things happened to me. I waited for everything to come down and then, at my leisure, steeped my heart into the joy and love that breathed out of every pore and sentence and word. I can see your love letters to God are making you more articulate, more open, more exuberant, more sincere. Your very heart is at the point of your pen and all you need do is to put it to paper and words and sentences. And paragraphs spill out from the cornutopia of your God—intoxicated soul. You sound as if you had just come from Tabor or from an assignation on Resurrection morn. Certainly not from a casual meeting with one who had been there. I am envious....

It seems to me that this whole summer from the very beginning was an adventure in God's fairyland—The dear loving souls that hovered about, every single one of them from Mary Inkrot to Mary Ann spewing out love like blowing whales and everybody caught up in a kind of ecstasy of sharing and loving that that turned everything to gold. You enumerated the special contribution of each one and you left no one out. It read like a litany of the Saints. And I am sure they are all close to them....

Your letter is so full of so many good things. I am not surprised that they are courting their finger on you for administration. You have so many talents and could be anything you choose to be. But then there is your preference and what you would be best at. I can see how you are inclined to move slowly in this. But this is just another thing for the Lord to decide. As far as "running things" goes you will certainly have your hands full this year. You have taken over enough for a dozen hands to do. I know you thrive on pressure and you will be able to handle them all without allowing them to get you down—providing that your spiritual life has room to expand. I will pray this year that the atmosphere of Blue Ash will be free of conflict....

My love to all your loves thereabouts as they gather around all agog for the opening of school. This extends even to Gráinne who I am sure is not there yet. As for you, I hug you, love you, cherish you. You are so loving, so kind to me, the one constellation in my sky, the main occupant of my heart. As you say, words don't tell it. All I can say is: Benedicat te... and a few words like I love you dearly.

Always,

Uncle Stanley

Enclosed recipe, handwritten on a restaurant place mat:

Carbonade a la Flammande (Belgian Stew)

    1 ½ lbs. round steak, cut in strips, 1 ½ inch by 1 inch.

    3 large onions, cut in slices.

    Soak strips of meat in wine and Dijon mustard, then flour and brown in 2 T of oil.

    Set aside.

    Add 1 dribble of oil in same spider. [The frying pan had legs so it could sit over the fire on an open hearth and was considered to resemble a spider.] Saute onions until limp. Put meat back in.

    Meantime, mix 2T of wine vinegar, 1T of beef nodules (or crush a cube), 1T brown sugar and 1 can of beer.

    Pour on above and simmer 2 hours.

    Thicken if you wish with 2T of water mixed with 1T of cornstarch.

    Add liquid from stew if you like. Pour it on. Mix.

    Serve with rice.

....

Letter 150

8:00 PM

My dear Ellen,

When I sit down to write a letter after dinner I usually end by tearing it up and putting it off till another day. Why I start one to you tonight is because I did not start one this morning when I was in such a fine mood and ready to pour out my soul into your little hand. Somehow or other I was sidetracked, principally, I believe, by a phone call from your mother who was anxious to find out how I was now since you told her of my hospitalization last week....

It is now the ninth day of May…
One thing I discovered in the hospital was a new way to meditate. Not a new method (they have all been used up) but a new posture. I couldn't stand the bed so would get up early and sit at my serving desk and prop my head in my hands and contemplate…Well I continue now that I am home and instead of sitting in my chair and dreaming I come out here to my breakfast nook and do the same… My mind stays alert and when I finish and am ready for Mass I feel as if I had accomplished something.

Although I must admit my memory is like a sieve and I have to go over and over the same passages in order to hang on to something to mull over during the day. And the next morning I might as well start from the beginning. Thus the price for old age, I suppose, but then my young age never approximated total recall. However the way, the method or the time involved, both you and I know the value of prayer. It is the without-which-not of our lives for unless we pray we simply become entrapped in a thousand snares and meshes that tangle us up and tear our hearts to pieces. Unless God is everything in our lives he is nothing much. And we know that even our appointed task can become an idol that takes his place. And when our appointed task involves people whom we have to love as we love ourselves we can be weaned away from loving God. It is a difficult world we live in, dear Ellen, and it can become a Merry-Go-Round unless we can skid it to a stop sign and listen.

Your mother got the impression that you were in a stew and upset but we both concluded that you were working too hard all together. You have got your fingers in too many pies, on too many wrists taking too many pulse-beats, sharing too many griefs. Thanks be to God we need only run the rest of this month into the ground to bring some relief. But I hope then that you don't have to leap right into a classroom immediately. You need the sun in Florida or the love of your uncle in Worthington to ease the pressure.

…Luckily your Retreat was a special grace at this time and brought you strength and the realization of just how unique you are and how uniquely loved by the Lord. And you caught a special view of the loneliness of the Garden when no one was there to watch with Him....

Have a great visit at home and at the wedding. It will be a special release for you. Too bad you can't stay longer... Peace to your heart and peace in your mind, I pray. God bless you dearly.

Much love

Uncle Stanley

On Women

> "A man needs to read *Catherine* now and again if only to show the male chauvinist pig what extraordinary creatures women are, to what heights they can aspire to and obtain, to keep in mind that her possibilities are unlimited!"
> —Uncle Stanley, letter 112

*D*ear One,

When I was in high school my dad suggested to me that I consider studying engineering. I asked him how many women engineers he had as colleagues at General Electric. He admitted, reluctantly, that he had none. I told him I did not want to be the first. I was more at ease walking in others' footsteps and supporting the others who would pave the way.

By the time I was a chemistry teacher, I mentored and advised bright young women who were the first (or one of very few) women in their own college engineering and pre-med classes. Now we have our first female vice-president. And Pope Francis has officially changed church law to include women as acolytes and lectors. Who knows what will open up next?

What I do know is that the women who went ahead of me: Mary, Elizabeth, Martha, Joan, Julian, Catherine, Teresa, Angela, Julia, Anne, Jane and dozens more, have inspired, challenged and supported me in my own life journey. And that the small role that I have to this day in cheering other women leaders on is a great privilege. And that I am so very grateful that, as a young woman, I had more than one man in my life who so valued women in theirs.

Unlimited possibilities, indeed!

Blessings and abundant possibilities to you!

Ellen

P.S. Write about a woman who has inspired, mentored, cheered you on. And enabled you to see unforeseen possibilities in your life or in the world.

....

Letter 112

Third Day of Lent
53rd day below freezing
My dear Ellen,

As usual it is bleak out. When it is bleak my mind leaps about like a bee looking for a rose to land on to imbibe its sweetness. As a rose, you fulfill every need. The fragrance, the honey of your dear self is suffused through the pores of my soul without even putting my lips to the cup. I need only to summon up memory in order to make you present. Thank God for memory. Catherine of Siena compares memory with the pitcher full of impressions which we obtain through our emotional life—fill it with nothing and the pitcher is easily broken or it emits a shrill clang if anybody knocks it. I have a whole pitcher full of memories of you so there's no danger of it being broken. Increasingly I imbibe strength by summoning you into my mind or, to keep up the metaphor, I grew intoxicated from memory of you.

For me it would be a perfect world if I could see and touch and talk with you about four times a year. Just think how the months would speed by if that were the case and as one came down to the wire how exalted one would be.

But we live in an indifferent world where such dreams are spun of gossamer and have no substance whatsoever. Better just to concentrate on Lent and the glory that leads to. Being the third day only, there is much time for reflection, much time to squeeze the joy out of whatever penance one can think up. And in spite of being seventy-nine, penance is still a matter to be reckoned with. One simply cannot accept one's advanced age for penance and let it go at that. That would be merely putting up with the common lot of man's disobedience and the Fall. Something personal, something special, is always demanded even if it is "just not turning your back on your own" as Isaiah said this morning in the Mass....

I think I told you in my last letter that I was reading Undset's Catherine again. A man needs to read *Catherine* now and again if only to show the male chauvinist pig what extraordinary creatures women are, to what heights they can aspire to and obtain, to keep in mind that her possibilities are unlimited! As I read my mind always adverts to you, the gifts that you have been given, the extraordinary gifts of mind and heart. Are they wasted in a lab or is a lab just a step on the way? Your capacity for holiness alone makes one almost resent the clutter of a too busy life. What is this fetish for education unless one is educating for God? Why not a change of goals that would be concerned solely with the holiness of others, the formation of souls, that would be dedicated totally to sanctification first and to degrees and competences after? Somewhere we have got the cart before the horse, to use a very homely expression. I look back on my own days and I wonder how I survived the course considering the ideas and ideals that possessed me. No wonder men falter on roads when the road was leading to nowhere. So I must spend my days in giving thanks in an almost slavish, obsequious way when I should be celebrating the glory in just being a son of God....

I wish you were here to help me with my crock pot. So far I have cooked four meals with it. I cannot say that I have been thoroughly successful any time. Yesterday I came closest, I think, with a jar full of chili con carne. It was palatable but with too much chili powder. Not that I put too much in, but everything was to be put in in layers and the chili did not permeate the whole but, I suppose, only in its immediate vicinity. And a glob of the "vicinity" was too sharp all together. But no doubt I will learn to use it by the time you get here to enjoy its fruits… Or its soups!

Your grandmother said she talked to you and you sounded very good indeed over the phone. She howled about the weather but who hasn't from coast to coast—including Cincinnati. I had to tell her in turn that I simply stay put and have no thought of going any place.

Charles called last night to say that Veronica is going to Florida so I am not to think of going to Caledonia until after the 23rd. Since meals depend on the Veronicas of the world I will not think of it. Moreover, I am content. I live in my house, with the reading light over my shoulder where I like it, where the sun floods in in the afternoon, where all is custom–run and according to Hoyle. I get in my car and go down to the Church and stop in usually at some oldsters abode just to spread sweetness and light. It is a good life and makes no demands on me. When I think of the agonies many people have gone through these past two weeks with a terrible storm they were not ready for, I am lucky indeed. NOT?

I must get this in the mail as the man will be walking up the street presently. My heart is in the envelope if you can find it and my thoughts are your thoughts. I love you very much and wanted to tell you so.

God bless you

On Zooming Across Time Zones

"I identify so closely with you that I seem to go through all the agonies, experiences, changes that you go through and wait with bated breath until you land on a branch with a nest neatly built and home—ready for a long stay...."

—Uncle Stanley, letter 167

*D*ear One,

It was more than a decade after Uncle Stanley died when I began to travel regularly for work. Crossing time zones via planes, cars and now cyberspace has become a norm. I must say that I love it. I love the way it brings people from different countries and languages and cultures together. I love exploring new lands and food, flora and fauna. And in the midst of such experience, I have found ways to be present to the dynamics unfolding in front of me, to zone out when I have a break (or am on an airplane), and to stay connected with those back home.

I have created a short ritual of leave-taking at the door to my abode when I set out on a trip. At the end of a Zoom meeting, a long workday or a full week on the road, I pause before logging off my computer and before checking in at airports. I breathe. I give thanks. It's as if I carry home with me and am ready to reconnect when the travel is over. In any case, it has made it possible to work remotely and to travel to wonderful places in the world even as I take my books, my journal, my knitting and my daydreams along.

Hoping you are well along the way or at home,

Ellen

P.S. How do you stay connected when you travel, to yourself, and to those you love? Or conversely, how do you stay focused on the present when you are traveling, on a webinar, or more busy that you'd like to be?

....

Letter 167

Thursday
My dearest Ellen,

Your letter yesterday somehow or other gave me a feeling of relief- from I don't know what? I identify so closely with you that I seem to go through all the agonies, experiences, changes that you go through and wait with bated breath until you land on a branch with a nest neatly built and home—ready for a long stay....

It's been so long since I wrote you a proper letter what with my neck in a sling and a complete upsetting of my usual habits. Since I wrote all my letters after I finished my breakfast in the morning it was all but impossible to get used to any other time. After breakfast I was all ready for a nap—an unheard-of procedure. No longer a slave to that necessity I am getting back into the groove just on time as I have a great many letters to write. But until this is written, and I will take my time, the others will have to wait.

I noticed you are travelling about in my old stamping grounds. If you listen you might even catch a sound of my old Klaxon. I knew Oak Park well having stopped at many a home looking for a lad from St. George's or St. Mel's High Schools who might be interested in going to St. Mary's. Up and down Cicero, up and down Oak Park Boulevard, up and down Western in hot pursuit of a prospect. After six weeks there I managed to produce just eight students....

I hope that you slip into your new environment like a dye gradually coloring and brightening all who live with you. They really have no idea how they are being blessed but that will come home to them very quickly. In the meantime I hope you are not home-sick but manage to keep busy. It does seem a long way to go to work as you must be up near Western Avenue and way down to 56th St… I will pray that Lois and Donna and yourself make at least a blessed trinity. It would be awful if you couldn't see eye to eye. But keep your eye peeled for an opening to Worthington. Count not the cost. Always remember that you are worth a whole flock of sparrows!!!!!

It's getting hot again so I will lay off for the nonce. But now that I know you are there, I'll be zeroing in on you. I will use the telephone number and don't fail to use mine. In the meantime may God love you dearly. You are so precious to me and I love you so much.

Your uncle

Uncle Stanley

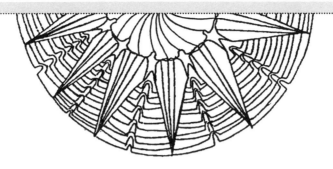

The Letters in Four Seasons
In the Season of Autumn

Autumn has always been my favorite season. As a child, I relished getting back into school and structure after a summer of leisure. In young adulthood, I chose quilting as a long-term hobby that would keep my attention on the present design in my lap. The complex layers of home, school/work and world hold together somehow and intrigue me with its patterns and connections. Autumn's anticipation and uprooting, with its color and coolness, stimulate my mind and imagination. Autumn's urgency and letting-go proffers a graced simplicity and playfulness. Uncle Stanley was in the autumn of his life when we began writing to one another. His delight in retirement was to stay actively engaged with more friends, family members, neighbors and parishioners than I could count. I learned from him, listened to him, laughed with him and always returned to my own busy life after a letter, phone call or visit with a deep peace that still sustains me through autumn's evolving changes in the pieces, patterns and pathways of life.

Delectable Delights

On Glee

"The house is empty and I have been roving all about hoping you are about some place. I have been setting everything to rights—pillows and blankets in your room, and *Alice* back in the bookcase. (You will always be associated with them now because you have handled them and loved them and pursued the Snark and helped the maids sweep the sand away…)"
—Uncle Stanley, letter 63

"Thanks be to God my eye seems to be clearing up. I can now read again with both eyes and the double vision begins about five or six feet away. So in the house I don't wear a patch. God is good, isn't he? You and I gleefully are aware of this and it brightens our day, smooths our going, excites our imaginations, warms our hearts and fills us with love for one another—Or don't you think? Anyway it must be the reason I love you so much."
—Uncle Stanley, letter 74

"I have packaged three of the most cherished books in my library and will send them on directly for you to grow old with."
—Uncle Stanley, letter 91

Dear One,

The word "Glee" will always be connected with my introduction to Lewis Carroll's *The Hunting of the Snark*. On my first visit to Worthington, Minnesota, as an adult, Uncle Stanley and I read it in its entirety, out loud and with great glee. We alternated reading sections of it in our own voices, almost singing, certainly laughing. It is a memory that the two of us would return to repeatedly, and the refrain tickles me still: "They sought it with laughter, sought it with glee…" mirroring the refrain in The Hunting…:

> "They sought it with thimbles, they sought it with care;
> They pursued it with forks and hope;
> They threatened its life with a railway-share;
> They charmed it with smiles and soap."

Uncle Stanley, St. Martin, Ohio, August 1973, Final Vows

Glee playfully nudges me beyond my too-serious-self into sweet joy. And, by the grace of God, it is at the heart of all of my dearest friendships.

I wish for you, dear friend, a moment of glee today. (A caution: Glee is fleet-footed, so be alert so as not to miss her visit!)

Gleefully,

Ellen

P.S. Sing a song remembered from childhood that brings you glee, still. Laugh. Dance. Remember the face of someone you love that shared the moment.

IN THE SEASON OF AUTUMN

....

Letter 63 (after my visit to Worthington, Minnesota).

My dear girl,

I have just eaten lunch—beef soup, grandma's brown toast (which I picked up in Madelia as we came through yesterday) camembert, and an orange. That all tasted like thin lentil soup in a concentration camp (I think) because you are not across from me (your dear face and quiet ways). It's been that way since I came home. The house is empty and I have been roving all about hoping you are about some place. I have been setting everything to rights—pillows and blankets in your room, and Alice back in the bookcase. (You will always be associated with them now because you have handled them and loved them and pursued the Snark and helped the maids sweep the sand away. Of all my loved ones, nieces and nephews, you are the only one whose mind and tastes run groovily with my own.) A light in the bathroom couldn't take the all night vigil and succumbed for lack of appreciation, like the comet Kohoutek, so I was down this morning for a replacement so I could shave the left side of my face. All it really did was help reflect my woebegone face and sad, sad demeanor over your departure....

I took your picture out and put it where I could see it as I passed to and fro and I have been passing to and fro. You can see the pad has been charged with your presence, baptized, and it will never be the same again. I don't know what I have done in my life to deserve you—your good, young, generous love. I can't tell you how I felt as yiu disappeared down the ramp Sunday afternoon—not sad, elated rather, that God had given me this gift for my old age, this token of his endless love—....

I hope you had an uneventful trip home, found your chauffeur at the gate and were heartily welcomed. I wish I could have been there to greet you. Now you are in the thick, lost between a Bunsen burner and a retort, no doubt. Let's hope not forever. Tis but the beginning for you. I know as your Ursuline adventure has much in store for you. I hope I'll be around to enjoy the journey.

God love you, Ellen, mine.
Prayerfully, affectionately,

Uncle Stanley

....

Letter 74

Fifth day of release
My dear Ellen,

…The day is perfect! My cleaning lady was here and after she did my chapel I said Mass while she finished the rest. It all looked so clean and shiny when she left—I proceeded to do my nails and wash my hair (that terrible burden)—One of the girls told me to wash it at the sink—And I remember in Dallas all the girls do that and make no great fuss or use much time. It worked fine! So I have learned to great truths this winter—a) wash your hair in the sink and b) prepare a grapefruit with scissors instead of a knife. If I live another ten years who knows how learned I will be in women's expertise. Maybe I could bring up a baby—an orphan, black preferred of course unless a prize from some unpronounceable town in Cambodia!

You will be overcome by this spate of verbiage I have been dumping on you this past fortnight. Do not feel any pressure to answer! Just be well, happy, holy and loving—I really don't need frequent assurances in writing that you love me. I'd bask in that awareness all day long! I don't think God needs many either—just so they are heartfelt when they are forthcoming.

And yours, when they come, are always that—I feel the touch of your pen on my heart.

I put a patch on my eye and drove over to Adrian yesterday afternoon and had supper with Marie. She is getting along well this winter. Came home and stopped at Adels for coffee and kind words. About 11:00 Pat Forsythe saw my light on as she came home from choir practice and got up nerve enough to buzz me. We had a lovely visit. She is a great lady. Thanks be to God my eye seems to be clearing up. I can now read again with both eyes and the double vision begins about 5 or 6 feet away. So in the house I don't wear a patch.

God is good, isn't he? You and I gleefully are aware of this and it brightens our day, smooths our going, excites our imaginations, warms our hearts and fills us with love for one another—Or don't you think? Anyway it must be the reason I love you so much.

Uncle Stanley

....

Letter 91

Dear Ellen dear,

It's a beautiful day this blessed day and I am so full of beans I just called Father Matthews to come in and drive down to Okobogi to lie in the sun and have dinner. So lazy am I today since I did not have to get lunch as Father Klein invited me down to eat with the children in the Cafeteria. The children still get hysterical when I come in and I am sure they don't know me nor do I know over a half-dozen of them. It is a throw-back, I think, to the days when the pastor walked in triumph and the children shouted (even across the street): "Praise be Jesus Christ, Good Morning,

Father"—a salute that I was brought up on in the Germanic emphasis of Mater Dolorosa School when I was a lad in Madelia.

You can see I am only writing this waiting for Father Matthews to arrive and when I have time on my hands I always think of you and sometimes turn to this machine to summon you vividly up and share with you my love and my thoughts. Cincinnati seems to recede from me but you don't fade one bit. I follow you all over that school and house of yours, listen to your voice, laugh at your laugh-provokers, pray in the pew with you, share a Manhattan and talk with your friends-good people all and holy and pleasing to God... I wish I could peep in on you and maybe stop long enough to hug you and shout the usual three cheers....

I have packaged three of the most cherished books in my library and will send them on directly for you to grow old with. [1. *The Path to Rome* by Hillaire Belloc, with the inscription: "JS Hale, 1924. May your conscience ache until you return this book to Room 24, North American College." 2. *The Hunting of the Snark* by Lewis Carroll and 3. *Through the Looking Glass* by Lewis Carroll.] The Belloc book I read at least seven times in my life and I still love to take it down and go off singing at the top of my voice with him as he slogged off to Rome. That book created a whole new genre of humor and travel books. Since then nobody can write a serious one and sell it out. It is possible you will not even like it- but at least it will be in the hands of one who cares. The other two you will go down to the grave with looking for a Boojum....

I came home Sunday night after two weeks in Caledonia where I basked in scenery, sunshine and solitude to my heart's content. I visited old friends in La Crosse and Winona and once again drove through old towns like Yucatan, Money Creek, Hokah, Black Hammer and Dresbach. The fall foliage was not at its most colorful but satisfied me more than a Kleist mural would. Fr. Charles is very busy sp [I deliberately left this typo, which should have been "so."] I had a car at my command to dash about and revel in the autumnal display. (I do wish I could type anymore without hitting that p so often when I am fingering for o.) I get tired of correcting the mistake and will leave them hereafter for you to interpret. No peripheral vision, no doubt....

...I rest content and simply wait with mouth shut and mind be at peace... Isn't the world a lovely place to live in- not the world but the earth and the fulness thereof!? The morning's paper today says that they are quite sure there is no life on Mars. Of course not! Only on earth, the beautiful, lovely garden of Eden that the Lord made for his friend, that he made to his image, man. So now NASA and the thinkers will soon discover man and from his flesh they may see God and the bounty of the Lord in the only land of the living. So the moon can go back to being green cheese again and Mars a red spot in the night sky and all the Snarks can turn into Boojums and you and I can sing Sanctus, Sanctus, Sanctus along with all the angels including the Guardians [the Guardian Angels whose feast is October 2nd] who will be dancing out into the liturgical dawn tomorrow morning. Whatever that is!!

You can see I get carried away at times but that is due to your own personality rather than mine. You are the sort of person I can engage in gibberish with as well as be silent with... You will be greeting all my friends for me, Phyllis, Regina, Carol, Gráinne—they are getting to be so many, so many beautiful people that God must love, mend and console them mightily. And remember the phone is there in the hall....

Love you,

Uncle Stanley

ON CULINARY AND POETIC ARTS

"I just typed two of my favorite recipes which you
will find some place in the depths...."
—Uncle Stanley, letter 96

> "This is a grand day and here I sit by my window watching the
> river of grass flow by, sun-dappled and shaded here and there
> by trees and flowering bushes. It could inspire one to poetry
> if Coleridge would be quiet and let one think."
>
> —Uncle Stanley, letter 164

*D*ear One,

Although my mother had a devilishly fun way of acknowledging our thirtieth birthdays it was not until I turned fifty that I found myself in a dark blue funk over an upcoming decade birthday. That summer I found myself with a free Saturday and spent it going through my whole collection of recipes, purging ones I did not think I would ever make and otherwise bringing order to the rest. At the end of the day, I had the sense that indeed, no matter how many dinners I hosted, there would never be enough time in my remaining years to prepare all the recipes I had collected. It was my first experience of feeling overwhelmed by my personal morality. I did get over it some weeks later though and before too long continued to delight in cooking favorite recipes and trying new ones again.

Once Uncle Stanley retired and moved from the Rectory at age seventy-four, he too began trying recipes, appreciating the gifts of produce from nearby farmers and welcoming advice from their wives. (His well-regarded cook, Marie, with thirty-plus years of cooking-for-the-priests experience did not seem to be intimidating in the least!) By the time Uncle Stanley was cooking for himself, I too was cooking for myself and we exchanged recipes from time to time. On one of my visits to Minnesota he made an especially delicious strawberry pie, made from donated strawberries he had stashed away in the freezer for a special occasion. He was so very proud of that pie!

As for me, when I was in my twenties and thirties I would have regular nightmares about having to feed a crowd made up of all the people I had ever known. It was an impossible task, perhaps a carry-over from the pressure I felt as the oldest in a family of eight children! But eventually, I grew out of that compulsion and loved cooking just for fun. Peach and Blueberry pie, Black Forest Cherry cake, and Grandma's cranberry Giftas, all sweet treats layered with color, texture and flavor, became perfect blessings for the end of a satisfying meal. A good spinach salad with mushrooms, mandarin oranges and slivered almonds is a favorite recipe to accompany a salmon-fettucine recipe with lemon-alfredo sauce that I brought to a Doyle family reunion decades ago but still love to make. On a recent trip to Belgium, I enjoyed one of Uncle Stanley's favorites: Carbonade a la Flammande (see letter 104 for the recipe) and renewed my intention to actually make this very traditional Belgian stew.

Uncle Stanley with his first baked strawberry pie, Worthington, Minnesota.

But with my current ministry taking me on the road and over the deep blue sea regularly, I don't have as much time and opportunity to cook these days. So instead of collecting recipes, I seem to have shifted toward collecting poems. My books of poetry in my library more than double my cookbooks. And the poems stored on my computer out-number my recipes three-to-one. Perhaps I have grown into a deeper appreciation for feeding souls instead of bodies, spirits instead of bellies.

But Uncle Stanley was a lover of both, fully enjoying both good food and a good poem, both sweet treats that I wish I could share with this dear Uncle of mine in my present life.

It is curious though that instead of bemoaning my mortality in these later years, I find myself longing for the life-to-come, even if I do wonder if a good recipe will be welcome. Of a good poem (if it would be welcome), I have no doubt.

My love,

Ellen

P.S. Find a good recipe. Make it for someone you love. Take a photo and share it widely, along with the recipe and perhaps a good poem too!

....

Letter 96

Monday evening
Dear, dear Ellen,

After the call last night (I had my phone fixed today) I decided to start all over. I just typed two of my favorite recipes which you will find some place in the depths....

It's just beautiful out this morning. The sun is climbing the sky and it is getting warmer outside. I shall go out today and shout in at a few old timers more imprisoned than myself, I have some good soup defrosting and this evening I will make some spaghetti as someone gave me a grand sauce for it. I wish you could share it with me....

Now the mail has come and a letter from Pat so I will go down and buy my ticket to Phoenix one way. It is hard telling how I will be coming back so I won't get a round-trip. I will buy it for next Monday which will give me a chance to clear my correspondence, my ice-box, my larder. I am now suddenly eager to go as I think I have put in all the winter that I care to for this year. Moreover one needs to see new people, absorb new ideas, new experiences, listen to new palaver or else fall into the doldrums. At least I find it so.

You can see that I need a refresher course myself from all I have so far written. No pizzazz, no umph! The only thing that rouses me is Trevor's Cardinal Newman. The second volume reads like an extraordinary suspense novel. What the Lord did to that man to make him holy! And holy he became and it is high time Rome does something about it. And all from his friends for his enemies and he had thousands—rubbing their Anglicanism into the Anglicans and they did everything to destroy his influence and thought nothing of totally blackening his character. Even when he withdrew into his shell and was content to bury himself in his Oratory at Birmingham they could not leave him alone. He was a terrible threat to them by merely being alive. And you can see what came of it in this century when those sane Anglicans are so ecumenically thirsty in our own day. And you can see what happened to the Catholics that did everything possible to lessen his influence among their own when the whole Vatican II rests on the foundation of his thinking. I read these in the early sixties when they came out but now I have more leisure and certainly am taking great gaudium out of their perusal. I will have to follow it with his *Apologia Pro Vita Sua* and his essay on Development. I have the first in my library and had the second. I must diligently go over my books. It may turn up....

Now that I have given up to you my dearest my Alice, I have to have recourse to other things to titillate my literary sense. And well for me for I am becoming eager to do Teresa's Autobiography again and Jorgensen's St. Catherine and even the Little Flower's biography. I pursue holiness just like a good Ursuline....

...Now time is getting short so I had better bring this to an end... It is this period after Christmas- all the way to Easter that is the hardest to get through—endless days without a good hold on the tassels of the Lord as he passes by. Time to climb a sycamore tree! But I'll continue this in my next....

God bless your dear self. I love you.

Uncle Stanley

Two Recipes, inserted with letter:

My Favorite Salad

    1 head of lettuce, broken in large bowl

    1/2 cup of celery-chopped

    1/2 cup of green pepper-chopped

    1/2 cup of onions-chopped

    1 box of frozen peas-uncooked

    A can of mayonnaise spread over the lot

    2-3 teaspoons of sugar

    4 oz. of grated cheddar cheese

    1/2 bottle of Bacos

Cover-refrigerate overnight-mix before serving.

Chicken Dish

I do this often with chicken breasts but take the skin off to avoid the fat. But it can be done with any parts of the chicken or with pork chops.

    Brown the meat and arrange in a casserole.

    Pour over a mixture of:

    apricot preserves (10 oz or more)

    1/3 package of dry onion soup (sometimes I use only a few spoonsful of chopped onions)

    a bottle of Russian dressing

    Foil it and cook at 350 degrees for 1 ½ hours.

Since this makes a lovely sauce, I only serve mashed potatoes with it and a lettuce salad.

IN THE SEASON OF AUTUMN

....

Letter 164 from Sun City, Arizona

My dear Ellen,

> "The sun came up upon my left
> Out of the mountain it came
> And it shone bright and on my right
> Went down into the mountain."
> —Adapted from the "Rime of the Ancient Mariner"
> by Samuel Taylor Coleridge

    This is a grand day and here I sit by my window watching the river of grass flow by, sun-dappled and shaded here and there by trees and flowering bushes. It could inspire one to poetry if Coleridge would be quiet and let one think. It is an ideal spot to lull and reread your splendid letter which contained all information, all wisdom, all love. I don't really know what I would do without you and your advice which as regards to your cousin Maura's essay was faultless. I shall follow it like a Parsee clinging to Zoroaster if Parsees are the devotees of Zoroaster and not somebody else. I wrote her a long letter before I left Worthington and haven't heard from her since but I will be hearing one of these days. Both Pat and Julia read it and the latter insisted on making a copy. But she promised not to spread it abroad. To let such a thing loose in a Convent would slam the door in my face, not?
    Your letter of recommendation is the very best and certainly the most fervent I have ever seen. The reasons Dr. Davidson enunciated for his appreciation of you were simply great—of your kindness, intelligence, efficiency, strength of character—this last displayed in your personal analysis of his own strengths and weaknesses. One can see it open up vistas for the future for you as not even a Catholic Superintendent of Schools could let you slip by without an offer to say nothing of the officials of other schools.

But the best part was the sympathy and generosity of Ceil who grasped your needs immediately and freed you to seek your future elsewhere. There is no doubt that the modern education of Sisters is going far beyond the Order's capacity to absorb and make use of. With the closing of the Academy in Brown County there is only Blue Ash and that seems to be filled adequately maybe for years to come. And so you look about you on your knees, fair girl, as competence and ambition beckon which may loosen ties and demand great faithfulness. In the meantime let us rejoice in your freedom to do so many things you have wanted to do. Too bad I am not home as maybe you could be summoned for a spell. But then maybe not. But I would love to be with you these days sharing your neat, feat ways....

I will not write a long letter today as I am deluged with birthday cards that I have been working on for ten days now and will continue to do so for days on end, I believe....

Much love now and God bless you dearly.

Uncle Stanley

On Birds and Beasts

"Ask the beasts and they will teach you; the birds
of the air, and they will tell you."
—Job 12:7

"The birds are shouting like mad and furnishing more music
than a stereo… Then there are the rabbits.…"
—Uncle Stanley, letter 118

> "Maybe there is a beast… maybe it's only us."
> —From *Lord of the Flies* by William Golding

*D*ear One,

Australia is burning from record-breaking wild fires. There are heart-breaking photos of the koala bears being treated for burns. Perhaps 30% of them may have been killed already. And perhaps a half-billion creatures lost in total.

Could a little bear reminding us of our own childhoods teach us, speak to us, shout at us and change our minds and hearts about the urgent action needed? What will it take for us to wake up, to do what we know we need to do to protect the beasts, their habitat, their air, their water? To say nothing of our brothers and sisters….

That's enough for today, dear.
With hope,

Ellen

P.S. What are the beasts teaching you, telling you, hoping for from you?

....

Letter 118 from Arizona

Monday
*D*ear Ellen dear,

I am sitting out here under an olive tree pounding away out of sheer exuberance of spirit. I was up betimes this morning and out here in the rising sun saying my prayers but I was driven in by the stabbing sun that can be as lethal as that gorgeous red oleander blooming across the way. But while we were saying Mass a breeze came up and changed the face of the earth. A little shade under an olive tree, a cooling breeze and we can ignore the sun although it has gotten up to 105 degrees the past few days. They say it has been unseasonable, but I know from the winter in Minnesota what that word means—while one suffers. But I am always ready to dive into some air-conditioned hideaway for relief. But I would hate to live in an air-conditioned world where one couldn't be caressed by a passing breeze or kissed by a vagrant zephyr (a smidgeon softer than a breeze). It would be sheer hibernation and would affect my nervous system, my peace of mind, my appetite and no doubt my pancreas or liver or something. So I stand on tiptoe, hoping that I can hold out, but ready for flight to cooler quarters should need require it.

I have just completed several letters home and have many more to answer-including yours, which just this minute arrived from Worthington and has sent me off into a dither of remembrance of how gracious you are and how loving and dependable. It was written while you were enjoying an odds and ends day yourself. Short, but filled with many good things like where you are going next year. I am rather pleased that you will not be too far away but accessible to Mary and Nancy and Maureen and Jill and all the others. I am sure they are all pleased that you are not disappearing out of their lives....

By the way I must explain how I happened to come here. Joe was put in the hospital for a twenty-eight-day cure and Pat called and begged me to come. So I am on my way to Dallas via Sun City. When I go thither I do not know but not for a few weeks, mayhap. Unless I am driven out by the heat that robs me of breath. (Just now the sprays came on that water the whole park. I am glad I moved under the lanai, for a few days ago I was deluged.) It is afternoon now and ninety-eight and the breeze has died down but I find that if I stay perfectly quiet and don't exert myself it is bearable. As you note I am not exerting myself. Never so when I write to you....

Tuesday
I am back under my olive tree and the weather has become cooler. I have my shirt off now and the sun is shining on my back. It is soothing and refreshing like a Coca-Cola. The birds are shouting like mad and fur-

nishing more music than a stereo. And many varieties. One gussy feller has a very loud Hi Fi, Hi Fi, and sounds like the forerunner of the Kings Horse. He only appears once in awhile but I haven't spotted him as yet. Then there are the rabbits that scurry across the grass in all directions and come quite close as if pausing for the time of day. You can see that this has become my world, quite different from Worthington where the school children were the rabbits and the brass bands practicing up and down the street my birds. The sun is the same on a hot day!

You can see I am running out of ideas. The sun congeals the mind and makes it sterile. So I will simply enclose my love and wish you well as you hurry on to the closing of school. God bless you.

Much love.

Uncle Stanley

On Great Books

> "I have started to dismantle my library. Is there anything you would particularly like out of it, poetry, prose, biographies etc. etc.? You name it—all you want."
>
> —Uncle Stanley, letter 132

*D*ear One,

For one of her graduations, I gave my niece, Ellen Brayton Porter, my complete collection of The Great Books of the Western World, which I had acquired from my mother when she died at age fifty-nine. There were fifty-four volumes, beginning with *The Great Conversation* and ending with *Sigmond Freud*. It includes a complete set of Shakespeare. Ellen was preparing for some kind of global job and the collection seemed a necessary resource, although I hated to part with it, especially volumes 1-3. Everything else could have been easily found in libraries. Ellen managed to take the set with her to her first big job in Washington, D.C., and perhaps has it now in her Paris apartment. After all, the U.S. State Department paid for her to move her things there and there is certainly ample room.

Another time, frustrated by the ten or fifteen unread books on the trunk at the foot of my bed, I set out to simplify. From then on, whenever I acquired a new book, I would give one away. And every book had to have a home on a shelf, even while lying in wait for its turn to be read.

I have three bookcases with fourteen shelves. There are 335 book-inches in total. I recently let go of some of my library to make room for special photographs, small objects and other treasures, including a clay teapot made by a now deceased friend, Greg Seigel, from Owenton, Kentucky. Half of one shelf is dedicated for transient books: books that have not yet been read and books that have been read but are waiting to be given away to a new reader or returned to their owners. I discovered long ago that I am only rarely inclined to re-read fiction, so it is a rare exception that I keep fiction, even though I always have a novel going. One of the three books of fiction on my shelf has twenty colored flags, marking passages I want to return to. Poetry books take up one whole shelf in my widest bookcase, with twelve by Mary Oliver, six by David Whyte and eleven by Moy Hitchen. Cookbooks take up three shelves in my narrowest bookcase (just fourteen inches wide!) which resides in the hall nearest my kitchen. There are lots of reference books and a few art books in my collection but not a single book of short stories. About a dozen have yellowed pages.

Although I have been asked to participate in several studies in which I reported what I was reading at various stages in my life and work, it never actually occurred to me to identify three or five or seven of my own GREAT books until I began this letter to you. And things could change. But, at least for today, here are seven of my own GREAT books, listed in the approximate order of my acquiring them:

- *The Prophet*, by Kahlil Gibran
- *The Book of Qualities* by J. Ruth Gendler
- *New and Selected Poems* by Mary Oliver (It's so difficult to pick just one of hers!)
- *The Solace of Fierce Landscapes: Exploring Desert and Mountain Spiritualities* by Belden Lane
- *The Art of Pilgrimage: The Seeker's Guide to Making Travel Sacred* by Phil Cousineau
- *Soul Sisters: Women in Scripture Speak to Women Today* by Edwina Gateley with art by Louis Glanzman
- *The Plover* by Brian Doyle

This task was not an easy one, and I have identified several that could easily be added to my list of GREAT books if I expand it someday to twelve or sixteen. And I do suspect that there are many books on my shelves that might be of interest to one or another of my own GREAT-nieces someday. Today, this exercise finds me wondering which books belong in your own list of GREAT books, at least for today?

Wouldn't it be fun to meet in a bookstore café and share our lists and stories over a cup of tea?

Until then, love to you, dear, and happy reading,

Ellen

P.S. Choose three or five or seven of your favorite books from your library and put them in front of you. Recall how and when this book came to you and if you have read it more than once. Imagine a nephew or a GREAT-grandchild finding it of interest and wanting it for his or her own collection of GREAT books.

Write a letter to the author, to a character you loved, or to a real or imaginary person you plan to give the book to someday. Or perhaps let a quote or paragraph from the book lead you to craft your own thoughts… Follow your muse….

....

Letter 132 from Sun City, Arizona

THE EIGHTH DAY
Dear Ellen dear,

Not the eighth day of creation but the eighth day in the valley of the sun where the green grass grows all around, all around, the birds sing in tune and the saguaro thrusts its mailed fist into the sky. I have just said Mass. Everything goes well except that the day I came my face fell and it has twisted my mouth out of shape. This has happened before and is called Bell's Palsy. Four to six weeks to cure so I can possess my soul in peace way out here where nobody cares whether your face has fallen on its face or not. I have been to the doctor and submitted to an $280.00 brain scan to assure the world that I didn't have a stroke. Curiously I have only one problem and that is drinking out of chalice. I slobbered at the Bishop's Mass yesterday at St. Clement's as he was out to thank his richest parish over their great contribution to his Fund for the Poor.

Sirach said this morning how even the sun could be eclipsed which reminded us that that is precisely what it was doing although the sky was quite overcast. But anything can happen in this country. I am astonished at its growth since I came out here first only about six years ago. Sun City is filled up and they are establishing Sun City West seventeen miles up the road. The severe winters lately are driving everybody out and I can appreciate their emigration because I had completely had all the winter I wanted last Monday when I took off. And it has been just as cold since with the snow piled up so that there is no place to put it. I think I told you before I left how the priests came out from all around in twenty-degree minus weather to celebrate my eightieth. It was really out-of-this-world and reduced me to tears. Last week I wrote every one of the twenty and told them what I thought of them and how I felt. That they left a case of Cutty Sark at my feet as a token of old decency has nothing to do with it. Their presence was everything....

...With my eye acting up I have read little since I came out. There is a raft of good books about and I see my old friend *Trinity* [*Trinity: A Novel of Ireland* by Leon Uris has 898 pages!] which I may resolve finally to tackle. It looks so thick and so formidable, I would rather read a short who-done-it.

By the way I have started to dismantle my library. Is there anything you would particularly like out of it, poetry, prose, biographies etc. etc. You name it—all you want. Mary Pat took my Sigrid Undset, Patsy the Graham Greene's, Charles a mescolanza [a mixture, in Italian...,] Mary Willette took some biblical stuff she is now teaching. Your mother wanted some old things and I would like to give her my Shakespeare but am reluctant to part with it yet. I will put her name in it so she can get it later when I am gone. It has everything, the sonnets, "Rape of Lucrece" etc. Or did you want it?

Lent is about to begin and I am not yet in the mood for it—but I have got the "face" to face it a lovely form of penance made to hand. But the ashes will make a difference and bring us all up short and put us on our mettle. So settle down for the long run to Easter and then we will let you out to celebrate the Resurrection of the Lord.

God bless now. I love you.

Uncle Stanley

On Quizzical Looks and Other Glances

"The robins are here and I saw several already. They seemed to have left Sun City about two weeks ago. I met one yesterday

> whom I am sure I knew. He looked at me quizzickly
> as if he had met me before."
> —Uncle Stanley, letter 178

Dear One,

Now that we are using video technology regularly for staying in touch, doing real work and finding ways to build community across hills, highways and households, I am pondering the gift of a quizzical look. What a wondrous thing to be able to see on the face of another! It is a gentle invitation to explain, a recognition that we may think differently from one another. Yet here we are with an opportunity for conversation. That the creatures in our world can also gift us with this acknowledgment of our presence is a joy: the reason that we have pets and visit zoos and explore nature. It is the sacred experience of being seen. Of being known.

Even though I cannot see you, in the literal sense, I'm imagining your own quizzical look! And wondering what you are thinking, exploring in that mind of yours....

Know I send love…

Ellen

P.S. Find a creature (or a friend or a blank page) and just be present to it long enough to notice its quizzical look, given to you as a gift today. What do you notice? In yourself? In the other?

IN THE SEASON OF AUTUMN

....

Letter 178

Holy Week Monday
*D*ear Ellen dear,

Snow, snow the beautiful snow! PFSST!

It's back again, that awfully pretty white stuff that poets hymned, skiers sung but old men like me have, I think, cursed for time immemorial. There may have been a few who did not have to go out in it who thought it pretty. But now the sun has come out and maybe will chase it in no time. In the meantime I am confined in the house because my car wouldn't start at the hospital on Saturday and I had to be towed. It is not back yet. But for two days I was driving it and found that I can do it very well if I watch the parking slots carefully. I stay away from the narrow ones as my left side is not to be thoroughly depended on....

It is great to be home and the weather that greeted me the same as when I left Sun City—seventy-two degrees. So I have hopes that the sun will return. The robins are here and I saw several already. They seemed to have left Sun City about two weeks ago. I met one yesterday whom I am sure I knew. He looked at me quizzickly as if he had met me before. The people have been wonderful and have called since the very first evening. I detest dishwashing of course but getting the meals so far has not been bad. I thought I had done a very thorough job shopping on Friday but there's no pepper in the house, no honey, no Kleenex—absolutely essential ingredients. But I said Mass with the boys yesterday morning and was at the penance service last night followed by a dinner in the rectory. Today I am anxious to be out but I haven't got my car back yet. It may come later....

It was ten thirty before I had breakfast this morning and now I am hungry (it is 3:15) so I had better forage something. Otherwise I will appear to be making a foodless Lent. And I can't leave that impression at all.

I'll be in touch with you by phone before your departure and we can finalize some kind of itinerary. God bless you much in the meantime.

I will.

Uncle Stanley

IN THE SEASON OF AUTUMN

Maps and Other Pathways

On Pride and Plenitude

"Let me begin by stating that your deep pastoral concern
for the people you have served over these many years
and are now serving at St Mary's was never more evident than
during our pleasant conversation of last Thursday…
that you were able once again to put the pastoral needs
of God's pilgrim people and of His Church
above every other consideration… To repeat what I said last
Thursday, you are in no way retiring from the priesthood.…"
—Letter from Bishop Watters in response to Uncle Stanley's request to retire

"I told the bishop I had not come for adulation
but for understanding."
—Uncle Stanley, letter 79

"Blessed are the meek for they will inherit the earth."
—Matthew 5:5

Dear One,

By now you know that Uncle Stanley continuously lavished me with his love in words, visits and support in ways that exceeded my wildest imagination. Those who read his letters at the time I received them warned me not to get too puffed up. And to always be humble.

Humility is a value I have tried to be intentional about practicing since the day I left home. That day, two of my younger sisters confessed how much they were looking forward to my leaving. It wasn't just that a bedroom would be freed up in my absence, but they would not have me to "boss" them around on cleaning day anymore. Ouch! Of course, being the oldest child has its challenges and one is to learn early on to carry the mantle of pride proudly! Of course, I knew more and better than they did that day. But ever since then, whenever I catch myself being cocky, arrogant and dismissive, my memory of that day comes back and I pray for the grace of humility, the grace to not know the answer, the grace to be comfortable in last place instead of first.

I was serving in a national leadership role in January 2002 when the *Boston Globe* headline announced: "Church allowed abuse by priest for years." The story had legs and went on and on and on for weeks, prompting more and more horrors of abuse and cover-up. It became apparent that clerical pride was at the root of it all, but in some ways, we were all complicit, putting priests on pedestals and looking away when they betrayed their vows.

It was in the midst of this exposé that our brand-new pastor welcomed ten neophytes into the Church, baptizing eight of them in our large font at the entrance of our new church at the Easter Vigil. Each entered the font by climbing the three steps up and then the three steps down into the water. Fr. Larry asked each one, looking directly into their eyes, straight-on, "Do you believe in God, the Father Almighty?" When the first man eagerly replied, "I do!" Fr. Larry responded, "Great!", and continued with conviction, "And do you believe in Jesus Christ…?" "I do!" "Great!" After the third question about belief in the Holy Spirit, Fr. Larry invited the man to kneel, drawing him completely under the water, three times, baptizing him "in the name of the Father and of the Son and of the Holy Spirit." (I was thinking: Could it possibly be that this one priest was one of the good ones? Not blinded by his own image and needs?)

As captivating as this part of the liturgy was though, it was the Confirmation ritual that sealed my own spirit with hope and joy. It was the lavishness of the chrism oil being poured over each one's head, without holding back, that drew my own tears. Such an abundance in a time of such scarcity. And, of course, the scent! That scent that stays with newly baptized babies for weeks. That scent that stirs up wonder and awe.

After pouring a profusion of oil over each one's head, Fr. Larry gently rubbed the crown and forehead of each person with no hesitation about ruining anyone's hairstyle. He then signed each with an oil-infused sign-of-the-cross and the words "Be sealed with the Gift of the Holy Spirit."

To witness such abundance, with the holy oil's scent pervading the whole church, was enough to make me believe that the Spirit is still more powerful, imaginative and loving than we know, even in the midst of so much scandal. It was enough to make me trust again that sacred touch could still be a part of our Catholic ritual, uncontaminated by sexual sin, psychological manipulation and clericalism. Not an Easter Vigil has gone by since 2002 that I do not remember the Chrism oil poured out that year and the hope in the Spirit that I reclaimed.

But humility remains an ever-present challenge, even in times of plenitude and hope. Letting go of prestige and pride is a constant challenge in the face of white privilege, #MeToo, and the often-misguided efforts in our country to Make America Great Again. Thank God that it is through the love of dear Uncles and late-night Easter Vigils that we can let go and trust a deeper Power than our own.

This has been a screed. But the sharing of it has been a grace. In Uncle Stanley's early words (from Letter 2): "Go slowly and do not get constipated less you lose the taste."

In hope,

Ellen

P.S. Write about a scarcity, an abundance, a moment of pride, or maybe a breakthrough of spirit. Keep the words private until a new day (or year) breaks. Or you get a letter that needs a humble answer.

······················

Letter 79

𝒟ear Ellen dear,

Only when I tackle a balky typewriter do I regret my unmechanical bent. This afternoon I have wasted hours trying to get the ribbon to flow freely through damns and narrows and sluices while writing a letter to Pat in Arizona who has discovered religion and prayer and the Spirit and is in need of simple encouragement and sane advice. I hated to send off the disfigured pages that I managed to put together but I did so and then concentrated my limited ingenuity on the entrails of this monster and I seem to have come up with a job complete. But don't bank on it. Prepare to offer up the outward signs of my inner turmoil should it decide to show a bit of temperament. Could I write in longhand like you do in the intimate script that creeps right into my heart? I would open up with some such paragraph as you did which was the very finest medicine for my soul that I have ever been given....

You thrive on reflection—you need time-space, you need freedom to pray, to exalt, to be gay, happy, holy so don't, I repeat don't, take on burdens that will give you no time for these. And don't go in for Zen, the contemplation of your navel, or become enamored of meditation that leads to nothing. Get out your St. Teresa and follow the old lady where she leads. You would identify with her sooner, I think, than the younger Therese. You have her temperament, her gusto for seizing the essential, her sane outlook. You must ready yourself for leadership and the practice you are now getting is excellent... Wherever you got your strength is a mystery to me. I look at your forbears and I wonder. And I do not hold them cheap, unworthy, or lacking. But I still wonder. It must have been some big offering you made when you were a child that was accepted—like the offering of Mary in the temple when she brought the turtle doves expecting to get her child, the first-born, back. She didn't but she never knew it. No wonder she pondered. I ponder too. Help me to ponder! Pondering can drive you gaga but now and again—beatitude!

Since the second paragraph it is the second day, Wednesday, and now I haven't been out for two days. A miniature blizzard with little snow has been blowing for two days and confining me to my room so I just finished supper—baked squash and pork chops done (baked) in a sauce. Delicious, with an apple and celery salad with a honey and lemon dressing. I wish you were here to share it with me. At nine I will have my coffee and at eleven I will go to bed. In the meantime I dawdle over this machine trying to show my love by dragging out this letter as long as my wits hold together. I am aware that I still must face up to Philippians, chapter 3:13-14. This I will do now and then finish it up.

To begin with I would like to say, maybe with blushes, something about the state of mind that moved me to go on Retreat. I was doubly anxious to go when I heard that it was Bishop Povish who was to be in command. I pondered about what I wanted to share with him for some time. The very first day I told him I wanted to have a talk with him when I was ready and he was free. He left it up to me. The gist of what I wanted to say is from Paul's letter to the Philippians: "What I used to consider gain I have now reappraised as loss in the light of the surpassing knowledge of Jesus Christ." Allow for a dearth of surpassing knowledge. I still found what I had accomplished as ashes in my mouth. It was my failures, my weaknesses, my failure to love combined with so much present adulation: a holy person, an excellent priest, a loving pastor ad nauseum.

I got little satisfaction from the Bishop. On the contrary he took off where the others left off. He said that he knew all about me and had heard of me long before we met on Sunday night. He recalled a Bishops' meeting in St. Paul where he and Archbishop Binz and Bishop Schladweiler and our own Bishop Watters were talking about the wonders a good pastor could work in a community. My name was brought in as a for-instance. How I had gone into one of the most anti-Catholic towns in Minnesota and in just a few years had turned around, not only the Catholics but also the Protestants. Until now it is one of the very best ecumenical centers in the State.

I told the bishop I had not come for adulation but for understanding. Then he really got serious and I went out of there walking on cloud nine with no fear of the future, no worry of the past. So you see Philippians is working for me: I can give no thought to what lies behind but push on to what is ahead. Helping to push are all those I love, especially you, the prayers, the comforters, the cheerleaders who come and go. The finish line is up ahead and with the help of all I can go singing to the gate.

It's wonderful to know you, love you, see you stretch your wings and glory in the good gifts that God shares with you. Wonderful to get such letters as you write and to be conscious of your presence always. You have halted the processes of nature, turned senescence into youthfulness, a humdrum existence into an adventure, an aching body into a soaring spirit. No wonder I love you.

God bless you

Uncle Stanley

....

Excerpt from Letter from Bishop Watters in response to Uncle Stanley's request to retire:

Dear Monsignor Hale,

Now that you are preparing to make the transition to the next level of priestly ministry which your well-deserved retirement represents, I find it very difficult, if not impossible to even summarize in one letter everything I want to say to you. Let me begin by stating that your deep pastoral concern for the people you have served over these many years and are now serving at St Mary's was never more evident than during our pleasant conversation of last Thursday... that you were able once again to put the pastoral needs of God's pilgrim people and of His Church above every other consideration. May you experience the spiritual joy of seeing the faith and devotion of the members of St. Mary's grow as a result of your unselfish priestly example and personal sacrifice for their holiness and happiness....

...As you review the remarkable growth of the faith community of St. Mary's since you came to Worthington in June 1943, you must admit that the development of St. Mary's School and the improved programs of Religious Education for all age groups, the enlarged vision of many of the lay people regarding their roles in the civic community as well as in the local, regional, diocesan and universal Church, and many others including the construction of the beautiful new Church would have been impossible without the effective cooperation of your associate priests, the skilled collaboration of the Sisters and lay teachers, and the responsiveness of all the people, the fact still remains that you as pastor have been the dynamic pastoral leader and visible center unity.

...your request for full and honorable retirement is now granted. To repeat what I said last Thursday, you are in no way retiring from the priesthood....

It goes without saying that I am most anxious to help you in any way I can. There is no doubt but what it will be somewhat difficult: both the idea and the fact of retirement. Bishop Fitzgerald used to say that the most difficult part was making the decision. Now that you have made it, I pray that you will have great peace of mind and soul; you have indeed spent yourself for Christ and richly deserve many years of happy and prayerful leisure.

With kindest personal greetings, renewed gratitude for your many years of priestly work in this diocese, and a request for your prayers, I remain,

Fraternally in the Lord Jesus,
Bishop Loras Watters
Bishop of Winona

On Getting Lost

"But the brash have the words and the media and the brave have lost their banners and their energy."
—Uncle Stanley, Letter 38

*D*ear One,

Not yet thirty and undaunted by the challenge, I moved to Chicago in late June, 1981. It brought excitement, terror and a little bit of cockiness. My housing situation was uncertain. My new role at Lourdes High School was bigger than I understood. And my friends were all staying behind in Ohio. Anticipating a trip further west to Minnesota at some point was a happy dream, but one well beyond the horizon. The whole thing was an adventure!

But my first time getting lost, just a few weeks after arriving in Chicago, was a major turning point. I was invited to a Friday night picnic with four of my Ursuline Sisters who were visiting on the far north side. After heading south from Oak Park where I lived to the southwest side and a full day of work, I made my way northeast to the lakefront during rush hour traffic. I hugged the right lane nearest Lake Michigan going north for another hour. It was a lovely ride, one where I could hardly take my eyes off the lake, its shimmering jewel color and dancing rhythms, its expansive horizon. But there was no time to stop. After a wonderful picnic and a heartbreaking goodbye to my friends, not knowing when I would see them again, I made my way south. With tears still running down my face, I let my little Pontiac direct me along Lake Shore Drive, trying to be alert for the ramp to the Interstate that would take me west to Oak Park. It was nearly midnight, too dark to read a map and not even the stars could help me navigate.

But I was a natural with directions, and I was sure I could find my way, even in the dark and without a GPS which had not yet been invented. The problem was that I mistakenly got on the northwest highway out of downtown instead of on the one going straight west! All the exits were familiar to me though from my in-depth study of the map before it got dark. Ashland was followed by Western which was followed by Kedzie. Then Pulaski and Cicero. Finally, I exited at Austin and turned north to look for Van Buren and Ascension Convent in Oak Park. It should have been right off the Interstate. Alas, though, none of the east-west street names were familiar! After a mile or so, I stopped to study my map. I discovered that I had somehow landed nearly ten miles north of where I thought I was. Turning around, I headed south and eventually found my destination at nearly 2 AM. It was a hard but life-long lesson that taught me the ways of Chicago, the ways of finding oneself along the way.

I never got lost again! The logical layout of Chicago streets became marked in my mind. I learned that if you knew where Lake Michigan was, everything was west. The friends I made in Chicago, the ethnic neighborhoods I lived in and the work-challenges I experienced there changed my life and I hated to leave when I moved back east. But I go west to Chicago and Minnesota whenever I get the chance and can find my way without a map!

There have been other times of feeling lost in my life. Even this morning, I wondered what this Saturday would bring and if I have lost my bearings. But somehow getting lost in Chicago so early and so late at night gave me a new-found confidence that all would be well. A Chicago friend observes that she thinks I have an inner rudder that not only keeps me from tipping over in my boat but helps me shift to a new adventure when the time is right!... I hope the same for you.

Be well, wherever you are…

Ellen

P.S. Do you remember a time of getting lost? Did it lead you to a new insight, to a new adventure, to a new-found confidence…?

....

Letter 38 from Worthington, Minnesota

My dear Teacher,

I was just thinking of the sheer horror of a world that demands that for two nights running I must be present at meetings on abortion. What a far cry from Al Smith, Mabel Walker Willebrandt, the Depression, the war. Amos and Andy and the United States Marshall of Dodge, Kansas. Mindful of my syllogisms and my neatly constructed developments of thesis this and thesis that that over the years dissolved into fragments and left me at the mercy of the modern world, I have come to this, viz, the careful scrutiny of a blob of immortality gradually taking on a head, a backbone, an eyebrow, a finger, foot and a heartbeat until he emerges into a man named "John" [Maybe Kennedy? Or maybe John Smith?]. But now the enemies of "John" who hate every muscle in his body but curiously enough love all North Vietnamese named Tye are out to destroy him. Not with napalm, a murderous weapon, not with bombs, the means of a savage, but with a surgeon's tool for $500.00. I have to dash about and inveigh against the likes of such human beings who love everybody, simply everybody, but hate "John."

"John," you see, is the enemy of mankind, the deflowerer of pretty women, the despoiler of happy homes, the up-setter of the bridge-table, intruder of the mixed foursomes, the robber of silhouettes, the receipt of guilty weekends, the offending party in every family quarrel. I would like to do something for "John." I would like to save him from this smear campaign, restore him to the glorious position of the first-born he once enjoyed. But the brash have the words and the media and the brave have lost their banners and their energy. But I do what I can and gradually there begins to assume a pattern of protest that just may reduce the legislature to panic and frustration. So they won't have to save the girl who was raped (in forty-four years of priesthood I haven't heard of her); nor the victim of incest (I never knew that she ever conceived). They will only have to have their noses rubbed into abortion-on-demand and come up with an answer. That will rattle their insides.

Wednesday afternoon
Now I have just returned from the doctor who was interested in the queer reactions of my gouty toe. He came to the conclusion that my medication is giving me more gout than it takes away. Like non-calorific Pepsi-Cola. So I am to take my daily abundance of pills, a pink, a red and a white one and add a grey and a blue and white. The color scheme alone will cure me of all evils even jealousy and alcoholism. But I just know the five pills must have some esoteric value in the science of numerology. Should you have time to trace it you might write your thesis on it for your baccalaureate. I must say that my health seems to be absurdly good although I do go lame as I walk the earth with gusto and elan. (In ten minutes I must call up Fr. O'Toole in Toledo to congratulate him on attaining the fine old age of seventy—the biblical age. May he live long in the land and work harder than he does and stop worrying over the younger generation whom, he thinks, are uneducated but actually are smarter than we are....

To get down to the meat of your letter and a fine sirloin it was I must say that I have never enjoyed a letter so much as this one from you. I liked everything about it particularly your declaration of love. It is wonderful to be loved and to love in return. You are such an honest beggar and face up to all the reasons that move you to action. The revue of your motivation that landed you in a country school house instead of in the Halls of

Learning was masterly and speaks eloquently of your character. You are a fine girl and I am delighted that I am related to you. I am happy too that you have a small cross to bear in the person of James Hitch. There are days I am sure when you could substitute almost any consonant for the first one and find that it fits. But he is there not to learn but to teach. The Lord arranged it. So that you would not forget that you are teaching persons and not simply making impressions on brains. You will run into many James' as time goes on.

The Sisters you teach with sweeten your adventure I see and you are lucky that you are all so compatible. Your lot will be thrown more with them this year than with any others, even Maureen and Dolores. That will help to broaden you, establish your equilibrium emotionally, weaken ties that were in danger of becoming too burdensome. But I am sorry to hear that Carol had to suffer a failure to identify. Something should be done to rectify this immediately lest harm befall. She is too much of a person to be lost in a card-index shuffle or in a failure of somebody's memory. Whatever will become of her ancestry? The Indians will bewail and bewhine in their tepees, damn the fork-tongued daughters of Angela, and break out the fire-water to invoke the shades of their fathers.

As for your Formation group which is determined to do something about prayer, I submit this by Julien Green: "Religion is not understood. Those who wish themselves pious, in order to admire themselves in this state, are made stupid by religion. What is needed is to lose ourselves completely in God; what is needed is perfect silence. Pious talk has something revolting about it." Maybe he is right. But he certainly would NOT love group dynamics. I have no ideas about Rahner but general ones which are the result of snatches of his writing. I have never read a whole book by him. But I do know that the younger men don't pray at all, at all. They do not give themselves over to silence. How can they with a stereo blatting out the beat…?

The new assistant is working in fine. He is a hard-working chap and is using his mind all the time. I think I disconcert him when I hold them to the line on things they like to ignore—like the price of catechisms, textbooks, etc. Nothing could interest them less. I have had to teach them to respect time, material things, lights, locked doors, etc. And meals that a housekeeper has spend hours on. But they catch on and strive to live within certain boundaries.

Since we had a late killing frost the trees are not near so colorful as usual. In fact I have been complaining that the autumnal colors are quite drab this year.

'Tis bed time. I shall not dream about you. I don't need to as you are very vividly alive to me. God bless you and *multo amore*.

Uncle Stanley

On Life Discernment and Decision-Making

"It looks as if you are getting deeper and deeper
into your work and probably will take over the principalship
next year. You do well to take time out to speak
to the Lord about these things. He certainly
is leading you someplace...."
—Uncle Stanley, letter 184

"Are all teachers? Do all work miracles or have the gift
of healing? Do all speak in tongues, all have the gift
of interpretation of tongues? Set your hearts on the greater gifts."
—I Corinthians 12: 29-31

> "The discipline of discernment demands a listening heart
> and a willingness to trust the deep inner call of Mystery."
> —From LCWR Occasional papers,
> Summer 2014, by Doris Klein, CSA

> "I returned home so full of the spirit of my nieces
> that I have decided to live until I am 110. You will be sixty
> by then and between/among you, you will have remade
> the world and I am determined to see what it will look like."
> —Uncle Stanley, letter 26

*D*ear One,

It was not until I was in my early thirties that I understood the ways and means and depth and power of discernment. I was holding in my heart and mind and spirit the question: what now?

Success and satisfaction had followed me to Chicago. The ministry of educational administration in a multi-cultural girls' Catholic high school was one in which I found great meaning, joy, and challenge. I was using many of the gifts I inherited from my mother and from my father, my life experience thus far, and what I had studied in graduate school and beyond. And yet something was missing. With the blessing of my community, I stepped aside from that full-time work for a year to ponder possibilities. My companionship of young women discerning about religious life was also stirring up a desire for additional study and formation in scripture and spiritual direction. Yet, I knew on several levels and with great clarity that I still needed to find a role that would provide financial support for my community and the space and time for me to continue learning and contributing in the area of educational administration. I was just getting started! Then during that year of discernment life got even more complicated. A Community and Organizational Development professor at Loyola University looked me straight in the eye and said, "THIS is your life's work." The THIS was serving as an external consultant guiding organizations through change and key planning decisions. And coaching leaders and teams. I protested, like the prophet Jeremiah: "Alas, I am too young!" Yet I knew he was right. I was indeed beginning to discover my life's work, even if I was not quite ready for it.

But it was at exit 215 on I-65 South at Rensselaer, Indiana, that the wisdom that would guide my discernment about what next was given. It was pure gift. An image of an intertwined rope appeared. One in which two thick cables, like those used on sea-worthy vessels were braided together. One in which two distinct ropes were so tightly wound together that there were no gaps between them. As I sat in the car that day, at an inter state exit halfway between Chicago and Cincinnati, I recognized what this meant. My life would be an intertwined path of outer work and inner work. A braided journey of administration and accompaniment. A public life in the world and a private life in the soul. That rope guides me still, forty years later. There have been seasons when one strand has been more visible, more conscious. But with practice using both in all of my discernment and decision-making since then, they have become so interdependent that I doubt that it would be possible to separate them. Not in my mind, nor my heart, nor my spirit.

I am wondering what strands of your life are becoming clear at this stage? And how that emerging clarity is guiding your own discernment? May your journey be a sea-worthy one! Or at least one in which a pause at an exit brings wisdom.

My love goes with you,

Ellen

P.S. Choose one or two important decisions you have made so far and walk backwards from them to that place of questioning what now. Sit with the stepping-stones that guided you to your decision. And write about what guided you. What mattered. And if there are any patterns emerging that might be your own intertwined rope drawing you to know and follow your life's path.

Letter 184 from Sun City, Arizona

My dear Ellen,

I just walked up to the corner and back again—the very first exercise I have taken since my first week here. The very first Sunday night I suddenly lost my appetite and became very weak. I finally went to a doctor and he thought that I had carried a virus down from Minnesota that caught up to me. But it really flattened me out and though my appetite has returned I have very little strength. I have written few letters and have been able to do nothing on my history nor have I yet any desire to tackle it… The weather which greeted me with 80 degrees the first week has been on the chill side ever since with off and on rains and little sun. I know I will come to life were the sun to take over for a spell.

It looks as if you are getting deeper and deeper into your work and probably will take over the principalship next year. You do well to take time out to speak to the Lord about these things. He certainly is leading you some place and already I sense that you are able to get along without all your friends of Cincinnati and are strong enough to accept anything the Lord wills. That is how it must be as I know well from what has transpired here the past three weeks. Nothing else counts except the Lord's Will….

With a new Cardinal-Archbishop Chicago ought to boom. [Joseph Carinal Bernardin was previously the Archbishop of Cincinnati and presider at my final vows.] I am sure great things will happen there. You must feel in the driver's seat with your own Ordinary running the show.

I am running out of steam so I will say good-bye. God bless you dearly. Much love.

Uncle Stanley

IN THE SEASON OF AUTUMN

....

Letter 26 from Worthington, Minnesota

My dear Ellen Doyle,

You're a love, a joy to the world. You add years to my life as if there were a whole new reason for being. I thought that I would get a letter of thanks off to you for your hospitality before you had a chance to write but here this morning is your loving note. I returned home so full of the spirit of my nieces that I have decided to live until I am 110. You will be sixty by then and between/among you, you will have remade the world and I am determined to see what it will look like. You have enough talent goodness, devotedness to bring forth on this continent a new state of religious dedication. I think you should be about it right now. The memory book you cooked up for Bert and her classmates furnishes the idea. The four of you and Bert (maybe her two classmates too, I don't know them) but certainly Bert for she is essential to the future of the world, should join together and make a yearbook every year consisting of your personal thoughts and hopes and accomplishments (growth in knowledge, holiness and goals)—and all with the view of giving order and stability and enthusiasm to the world you live in and the world you will affect. Such a memorial could give the individuals a tremendous prod to grow and grow. Of course I did not have enough time with Carol and Dolores and someday I must remedy this. Sandy I feel I know well and her spirit gives balm to her friends. I do hope that she will not have to go on suffering from her back but that relief may come quickly. (Nothing for the two of you to do but to come to Worthington whence I can deliver her to Canistoga.) I think I know Bert well too although I had no chance to talk to her but something of her spirit went forth and kindled a like spirit in me. Carol's romancing slays me and what a gift to enliven the world she lives in. I do hope that Dolores and Father Klug end up by converting Brown County. Or at least by loving each other.

I am glad you are mellow and happy and calm and contented. You sound as if the angels had been talking to you, telling tall tales of a time when the world was young and God played in the world, delighting to be with the children of men. Or as if you were suddenly immune, insulated from the world of fear and frustration, enjoying the lull that comes before the storm. When the storm comes let us know as I would like to take a stance in the exact center. There I can send out cheery messages calculated to vex (isn't that a fine old word) and harass you and cause you to twitter and twist. I think I can aggravate any serious condition.

At the Doyles all was serene. I was only asked one question: Did I think that Ellen would persist in her vocation? I answered that they ought to know the caliber of daughter they had and of all things I was sure that she would. Papa said to Mama, you see, these are exactly my sentiments. They seem to be looking towards Carolina for the future and their vision seems to be compounded of many things that I have no desire to probe. I enjoyed my visit very much, had two excellent meals, two excellent sleeps and went out to lunch at the Stranded Ship. It was delightful. They told me that they had entertained you there and I strained to catch your aura but the atmosphere was too alcoholic….

Now Marie is gone to Chicago and we batch it the best we can. [Marie had been the cook at the rectory for decades. Her culinary expertise was known throughout the land!] She left on Wednesday and fixed up a pan of calves' liver for me to cook in a pan for supper. The others do not like liver and were to be gone for the day so it was a good opportunity for me to enjoy this delicacy. Everything went fine until I came to cut a wedge of pie for dessert. Then I noticed the frying pan needed soaking so I turned on the water in the sink and proceeded to soak it. I went back to the breakfast nook to eat my pie and read and when I came to about a half hour later I looked up to see a flood of water surrounding me and out into the hall and into the office and out to the entry way and as far as the dining room door. God help us all. I couldn't find the sucker over at the school so had to tackle it with a mop—a MOP mind you. Put humpty-dumpty back together with a mop. Fill up a twenty-gallon barrel with a MOP! After an hour, I was licked. I sent out a call for the sexton and he came after a half hour and found the sucker and went to work. By 9 PM I had to leave to say the prayers for a poor man dying at the hospital. I came home licked, frazzled, exhausted. AND all for a plate of liver! Or was it the book I was reading?

Now I must be off and get ready a little sermon for the Knights of Columbus who are going to install their officers at the offertory of the mass I will say for them at 8:00 PM.

You are a dear girl Ellen Doyle and I love you very much

Your uncle

On Retirement

"…every day it comes to my mind how good the Lord
was when he planted in my mind the firm conviction that I would
just wither away were I to choose any other place
but Worthington for my retirement."
—Uncle Stanley, letter 172

"After 30 years it is time to say Good-bye to you. I may be
around, who knows how often in the future, but for all practical
purposes this is the day of departure.…"
—Uncle Stanley, letter 54, excerpt from Farewell Sermon to St. Mary Parish

"She came to our town and started to do her real work."
—From "Grief" in *The Book of Qualities* by J. Ruth Gendler

Dear One,

I was just forty-seven years old when I left Chatfield College after eleven years of service as its president. People assumed I was retiring. But alas, nuns do not retire. Instead, we discern about what's next.

After a full twelve-month sabbatical that year after I left Chatfield, I was back in a leadership role and have been ever since. But, even as my present ministry becomes less intense, I am not considering if the time has come to retire. Instead, I draw on the grace of that sabbatical and merely listen and pay attention to the question: "What is mine to do? What is my call at this time?"

Uncle Stanley, Worthington, Minnesota, celebrating his 50th Jubilee, May 1976.

I am noticing a shift though from outer, public work to inner, more spiritual work. From doing to being. I have more time for writing, for cooking, for reading, for breathing, for connecting with people. And I am grateful that I am not withering. It is a sweet blessing, along with my health, new friends, and the sense that the world needs my gifts, still.

And I have time for you. That has been another sweet blessing: to imagine you, as the reader of this letter, where you are, what you are doing, what draws you to and away from work. I have a sense of your presence, even across miles and time zones, confirmation, I think, of the mystery of the communion of saints as we make our way through this precious pilgrimage of life. Thanks be to God!

Blessings,

Ellen

P.S. My younger sister Jeanie retires in just a few weeks, after counting down the days and hours for many months. Today she starts a new complicated knitting project. Tomorrow she finds out if she and her husband will get the new puppy they are hoping for. She is very excited! Think of someone you know who is retired. Or slowing down. What do you see in that person that is attractive, enticing? What do you dream for your own retirement or slowing down?

Letter 172

My dear love,

I emphasize the love in order to remind you that there are many who love you and whom you love dearly but they do not happen to be in Chicago. So we try to substitute by visiting, writing, calling so that you will not feel lost in your new world. I know precisely what you mean when you say that you have many charming new acquaintances, but no one has showed up that you can share yourself with as yet. The reason why I know is because every day it comes to my mind how good the Lord was when he planted in my mind the firm conviction that I would just wither away were I to choose any other place but Worthington for my retirement. It was the custom always for the old pastors to get out of town, to leave all their familiar surroundings, all the people who loved them and whom he loved and go to some apartment in a larger city or to a home for the old. I simply shudder when I think how close I came to that choice. I was prevented only by not being able to select the right spot. So I got up one morning with the decision made and after Mass and breakfast I set out to find a house that would welcome me. Before night it was all settled and here I am living happily ever after. And my loves come in my door and invite me to theirs and they are not decreasing but increasing....

The paper did not come this morning as we have had our first blizzard—a very sudden explosion out of the West that came last evening. It has stopped snowing but is still blowing so I don't know whether I will get out today. Just as well as it will give me the incentive to start my Christmas cards. Last evening I counted the addresses in my address book and they numbered 252. When I finish them I have all the locals and all those people from whom I get cards who are not in my address book. Maybe the traffic will be diminished this year because of the price of stamps. This never deters me for some reason or other but I have other ways of conserving, e.g. not smoking, drinking conservatively, driving less, avoiding steaks, movies, pictures, records etc. But I eat a lot of popcorn! Sic!

Your mama wrote me a letter this week and sent me a picture of Amy after a volleyball game. It seems that they came out third in the State. Mama feels great and is vastly content on her estates. But the best thing that ever happened to her is the Retreat she made last spring. She is really a new woman. Papa seems to be thriving.

I must write to Mary Kay and give her a stirrup up as her big day approaches. I am very happy for her. And I hope she lives happily, ever after. Sorry about Joe: to have a spinal fusion when so young but he is lucky to be out of the football wars and can look forward to something more intellectual to earn his living and living for his bride.

I enclose the schedule which you must take advantage of should the opportunity reign. It's on Ozark Airways and the planes will be small but the safest there ever have been. If no time for me to buy a ticket—pay out and I will reimburse you.

We are all going to Tommy's in Madelia for Thanks Day. Charlie hasn't made up his mind. After a few hours of company he cannot take it any longer emotionally. Doctor Fitch says there may be withdrawal symptoms coming off cigarettes.

God bless you dearly, my dear love and walk in the Lord....
Thine

Uncle Stanley

IN THE SEASON OF AUTUMN

....

Excerpt from Farewell Sermon to St Mary Parish

After thirty years it is time to say Good-bye to you. I may be around, who knows how often in the future, but for all practical purposes this is the day of departure... A certain loss of health, of hearing, of energy, the infirmities of old age, to say nothing of the good of the parish or the clamor of youth from below-have brought us to this hour....

I have no intention of reviewing the work that has gone on here these thirty years. That would be dangerous—we would be too concerned to pick out those highlights that mark the passage of every pilgrim on his way to dusty death, that would in the end amount to nothing but self-praise. We are far too well aware of the low spots that marked our passage—failures of personality, of kindness, of pastoral care, of love—thoughts which even now erode our peace of mind, disturb our prayer... I am truly appalled at all the opportunities missed, at the failures of communication and understanding and sympathy along the way. To off-set this feeling of failure to fulfill an office in the way you have a right to expect from your pastor—I am consoled, as I go, by the truly enormous response given by the people over the years....

To whom am I grateful, for what am I grateful?—EVERYBODY, EVERYTHING! Two things and I must cease:

I always thought that a pastor who dared to burden the people with debt—should see that it is paid off. This could be one of the reasons for my dilatory departure. We still owe $47,500.00. May I ask you to take care of it as you have in the past? I can't wait.

Second—I don't know who the new pastor may be. Whoever he is—he will be different in personality, in method, outlook, emphasis. PLEASE cooperate with him fully and never present him with this facer: Father Hale did it this way—Father Hale could have been wrong.

On Aging

> "It [Thanks Day] will be a brave effort to display Americana and Christiana on the level of a middle-class parish without any problems except a sentimental pastor, getting deaf and sliding, sliding down the banister of time into the ashcan of a hall closet kept by Ursulines for old and discarded priests. Mind you, you young snippity-gibbet, I don't mind consorting with Ursulines but I do fend off with earphones and guile any hall closets and even any ash cans...."
> —Uncle Stanley, Letter 3

> "For age is opportunity no less
> Than youth itself, though in another dress,
> And as the evening twilight fades away
> The sky is filled with stars, invisible by day."
> —From "Morituri Salutamus" by Henry Wadsworth Longfellow

*D*ear One,

I read an article this week about a nun who started running at age forty-seven and intends to complete one more triathlon at ninety. Meanwhile, I struggle with how to respond to friends who question my commitment to my work, my international travel, the energy I put into living as I begin my seventh decade. I am alive still…and glad to be writing to you.

The daffodils bloomed this week, though, this year, they are less perky than usual, having bent to the alternating freeze and thaw. As long as my work does not keep me from being limp, folding to the demands of work and travel, as long as it doesn't keep me from writing, from learning, from reading, from discovering something new in the dress of youth itself, I will continue to say "yes" to those opportunities that I sense my being called to. With feet planted and eyes star-gazing toward the life-to-come, I will take one year, one month, one day, one sacred minute at a time.

Be well. Be alive. Be open to what is yours to do in the world, no matter your age.

Blessings,

Ellen

P.S. Write about one or two opportunities in your own aging, a lesson in humility, a dress you loved as a child, or a night of star-gazing you remember…

....

Letter 3 from Worthington, Minnesota

My dear Trivial Ellen,

It is the night before Thanks Day and I have just put on a small piece of paper big thoughts that I hope to convey with unction to the thousands that come out tomorrow for the Mass. It will be held at 9:30 AM and I am sure we shall pack the roof beams and whatever other nooks and crannies that were left over after the architect drew the straight lines. There will be…the passing show of trumpets and guitars and mandolins that will accompany such a stirring offertory as God Bless America and such a meager bleat as the "Star-Spangled Banner" for a pre-recessional. Besides there will be Papal and American flags in the offertory procession, Red Cross nurses, sailors from the fleet in Vietnam (come for the purpose), a young courting couple (who will be married Saturday), an old couple with their ancient memories, youths with footballs, bicycles etc... It will be a brave effort to display Americana and Christiana on the level of a middle-class parish without any problems except a sentimental pastor, getting deaf and sliding, sliding down the banister of time into the ashcan of a hall closet kept by Ursulines for old and discarded priests. Mind you, you young snippity-gibbet, I don't mind consorting with Ursulines but I do fend off with earphones and guile any hall closets and even any ash cans....

After the Mass I shall diddle away an hour or two and wait for your Grandma and the Schaefers to descend with blessings on our house. [Patricia Schaefer was J. Stanley Hale's youngest sister and, at the time, lived with her husband Joe in Owatonna Minnesota.] Squads of Quinns were also invited but will hole up in Fairmont where three generations will sing and play and clap their hands whereas I was able to handle only two. [The Quinns were the grown children of J. Stanley Hale's sister Lily Ann.] We shall broach in reverent awe (God thought of everything) a bottle of red Volpollicella which some people say blushed one day at a compliment of Mother Mary but which I say began to bleed out of sympathy for the plight of the Holy Innocents. At any rate, as everybody knows, it was baptized in the presence of Michael, Gabriel, Raphael and all nine choirs of angels, a leprechaun or two and a lion that roared out of sheer exuberance of spirits. Then we will proceed to demolish that totally overrated bird known in this Turkey Capital of the World, King Turkey. Overrated, because of its lordly demeanor and its horribly raucous voice, its spread of feathers (trying to imitate the peacock) and that little wormy thing dangling from its crest that always reminds me of a deposed Emperor of Lilliput or one of those terrible Gorgon girls whose hair turned into snakes. But of course there will also be pumpkin pie etcetera, etcetera, etcetera....

I am certainly glad that you enjoy your innumerable parties. You enjoy them even before they come, not? Like Friday the Thirteenth and

Halloween. You sound as if they come every month. Why, lass, you may have to wait years for another party at the rate you have them. But I see you enjoy simple things. I think that is a sign of a good religious: things like mail, and big bathtubs, and malted milks, singing practice and a peaceful chapel. I thought that one had to be as old as I to enjoy simple things. I find now that I revel in an hour of reading before bedtime. (I really can't stand TV!) I like to talk to small girls and people who are not quite right. (I have had a lot of practice at this lately since I have been up to Willmar four times in the past month.) I like to walk downtown and wave at everybody and pass the time of day. I like moons when they are lying on their back and the smell of horses and Dublin Stout. But I am delighted that you like people more and more as their real personalities come out and the sweet secret, the deep secret, is disclosed. That, my dear, is the sign of holiness.

I might as well start another page since I have another twenty minutes to give to the Ursulines. After that I will go upstairs and read Gene Kennedy's new book, *Fashion Me a People*. [Eugene Kennedy, then a Maryknoll priest, had grown up in Fr. Fagan's parish on Long Island.] He amazes me. I meet him once or twice a year (in Chicago or Long Island). His writing is crammed with neat phrases and he is writing some excellent common sense in these days of confusion, which I love. I might suggest that it is always delightful to a confused person to see the times catch up with him. Of course, I can sleep over tomorrow and you probably can too. (May the Name of the Lord be blessed!) Let's dream a fine dream together like Jacob and the ladder with the angels skipping up and down. You be the angel. I'll be Jacob. I like angels.

Hasta Usted Espanol? Spanish needs a palate but mostly lips and tongue. Fill up your mouth with frijoles and you can talk like Don Quixote—or maybe Sancho Panza. Philosophy, you say, is okay. What is that word the Victorians used to call young maidens who liked such things as philosophy? Oh, a Bluestocking! [An intellectual or literary person; and since the 18th century, a woman who was so.] Are you such? Or maybe just a young girl who can't pick out the right Epistle, who loves her newly discovered world, the winter's snow, chapels (full or empty), sleep-overs, mail, feast days, Compline, Lauds, and Vespers, brothers and sisters and the good God.

Yours, my dear,

Uncle Stanley

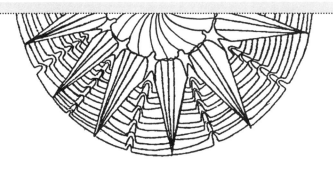

The Letters in Four Seasons
In the Season of Winter

Winter is the season of witnessing: witnessing what has been accomplished, witnessing the diminishment that comes with age, witnessing what matters in the end. The light is low. The nights are long. Some days dawn frozen with grief and loss. Uncle Stanley, in his last years, would escape Minnesota winters to be with his sister Pat in Arizona. In winter, there is "be-ing" time for writing, reading, singing, connecting, dreaming, waiting. As I write this, a pandemic comes like a fierce winter for our world. It thrusts us into seeking shelter even as we cannot know what lies beyond the mist around us. Winter is a taking-stock season. It lurks at family bedsides, national borders, and social and personal chasms that divide us from one another. This sacred season, like its sister seasons before it, invites a wrestling with mortality and faith. It promises transformation and fulfillment. I am in the winter season of my life most days now. And grateful for its flexibility and expansiveness and wisdom. With holy tenderness, winter deepens my attentiveness to those thin places where we briefly glimpse the threshold between life-in-this-world and life-in-mystery. Uncle Stanley is there on the other side, with so many of my dears. And that is enough.

Keeping Vigil

ON FAMILY TREES, BRANCHES AND ROOTS

"Three things I must do before I die: One, to write out the family tree. (Many are asking for it.) Two, to write and have printed a leaflet on the windows in our church. Three, to write the history of St. Mary Parish here in Worthington especially the last twenty-seven years of it. I have it all down in the Sunday Bulletins I have printed for twenty-seven years and have saved. So I'll take your advice and get busy on the TREE first. But you may tell Anne that County Monaghan is the home of the McGinn's and County Armaugh of the Hales."
—Uncle Stanley, letter 39

"It is hard to believe that I have come into this peace and simply do not know what to do with myself. After all the busy-ness with cards and letters I thought I could get my fingers at long last into the family tree but just now have no appetite for it."
—Uncle Stanley, letter 144

"I've come from the lacing patterns of leaves, / I do not know where else I belong."
—From the poem "Ancestors" in The Carrying by Ada Limón

Dear One,

Uncle Stanley was a second generation Irish-American. He kept in touch with cousins on his father's side from the time of his studies in Europe until he died. The stories and address list he gave me were both invaluable

Extended Hale Family, 1948, Madelia, Minnesota. Sr. Julia in the center, with her parents on either side of her; Ellen's mother, Mary Catherine Hale Doyle, just behind Sr. Julia; my Grandmother, Ellen (Nell) Hale, just behind and to the right of Mary Catherine; Ellen's grandfather, Desmond J. Hale, just behind Fr. Joe Hale; Uncle Stanley, right of his dad, JP Hale, my great-grandfather.

....

when I went to Ireland myself for the first time thirteen years after he died. I remember looking out the plane window that day when approaching Dublin and feeling like I was coming home. I was going to meet "my people" and walk on "my land."

For one family I visited I just had a town and county to guide me: Carrick-on-Sur, County Waterford. No street. No phone number. Because of my letter to them a few weeks earlier, I hoped they were expecting me on the May Sunday I would be passing through with my dear friend Anne, whose family had left us the money for the trip. Anne had explored her own Maher and Fallon roots in Ireland with her parents several years earlier and she had a good sense of what the discovery was like. But despite her confidence that we would find them, I was still worried. I need not have. Just after Sunday church services, we arrived in the town and stopped at the local pub where several men sat outside chatting and observing the comings and goings. We asked about the Mooney family. "Aye," they said, "and ye shall find 'em up and around that bend in the road. They'll be waiting for ye!" Of course! It turned out that the extended Mooney clan had gathered in anticipation of reconnecting with me, one of their own branches and they had a lovely plan for an all day visit, complete with midday dinner, and lots of storytelling and picture taking. It was a pure delight! And built a relationship that was rekindled on my subsequent trips back to Ireland.

My siblings and I are so lucky to have all four family trees from all four of our grandparents. There are branches that are lost, but also roots that go back centuries (the Hale family has one branch that Uncle Stanley traced to 1648)… My nephew Preston, who will be married soon, has an interest in our family genealogy. Who knows what twigs (and stories) he may discover!

Perhaps you too are exploring your own roots, branches and twigs… Be on the watch for clues that will lead you just around the bend….

Peace to you and your people,

Ellen

P.S. Who are your people? And where did they hale from? Write about a favorite story…and pass it on.

....

Letter 39 from Worthington, Minnesota

My dear girl,

…I awaited your letter with the utmost interest and I was astonished and delighted that it was post-marked Wilmington and that you were able

Ellen with Desmond J. Hale, Uncle Stanley's brother and her grandfather, Madelia, Minnesota, about 1958.

to get home for Christmas. I detected a compassion and love that is almost totally objective and that demanded no decisions on your part whatsoever. It seems to be that you are growing into your life of service and dedication, shall I say, so relentlessly, that you are not to be side-tracked by any demands others may make on your life. I note this all along the line. People who meant so much to you only last year are doing their own thing without any overwhelming interest from you. Amazing how the present, wears away the fabric of the past.

Friday-3:00 PM
…Since you do not write so often anymore being so busy with a thousand and one details of teaching, living, communicating etc. I note an amazing new stride as if you had seven-league boots. You don't dramatize trivia; you face up to things; you have taken charge of Ellen; you act rather than react. And I note that you are discovering that deep down there was germinating beneath all the apparent reasons for joining the Ursulines, the real reason. This is a matter that has caused me more wonderment than anything in my life. I seemed to have had no reason for what I did when I decided to become a priest. Even in the Seminary I seemed to be acting a part. Even when I was faced up to making final choices I didn't seem to dig it the way I should have. But gradually the thing came alive in my mind and I look back in fear that on any given Tuesday I might have taken the wrong turn. And what kind of life could have been mine had I not become a priest. I simply can't imagine being anything else. All other

jobs, professions, vocations would have stifled me. Had I quit I probably would have drifted into marriage and had a wife support me. Someone was constantly plucking at my sleeve and I look back in horror at a few plucks that didn't mean much at the time but would have sent me straight on into disaster had I not heeded them.

…So you grow and grow and grow and daily become more Ursuline-ed. I would love to get down and see you but you are very busy I know and have no time to visit. But remember the phone and the number and call often and charge it to me.

Three things I must do before I die: One, to write out the family tree. (Many are asking for it.) Two, to write and have printed a leaflet on the windows in our church. Three, to write the history of St. Mary Parish here in Worthington especially the last twenty-seven years of it. I have it all down in the Sunday Bulletins I have printed for twenty-seven years and have saved. So I'll take your advice and get busy on the TREE first. But you may tell Anne that County Monaghan is the home of the McGinn's and County Armaugh of the Hales.

God bless for now, love,

Uncle Stanley

....

Letter 144

The Day before Christmas
My dear Ellen,

It is hard to believe that I have come into this peace and simply do not know what to do with myself. After all the busy-ness with cards and letters I thought I could get my fingers at long last into the family tree but just now have no appetite for it. I would rather write to you so that you might get word during one of the days of Christmas. Suddenly this morning after all the heat and the fogs of the past five days I went out to the Mall to do my Christmas shopping which is always done in a trice. It was chilly and will become more chilly as the day advances. So long as it doesn't snow I will accept whatever comes. Just now there is not a spear on the ground and I hope nobody is praying for a White Christmas—as if one needed atmosphere to appreciate the great Feast!

All I need to do is to envision the travelers on the road today coming down from Nazareth—Joseph leading the little ass on which Mary sits as comfortably as possible although I imagine her clumsiness moves her to get off and walk quite often. They are not far from the end of their journey now—at least they hope to get in by night-fall. Being common folk they don't anticipate a great deal of comfort at the end of their journey. They don't think in such categories as Holiday Inns or Ramadas—a cheap caravansary will do where they can get fodder for the ass and some kind of shake-down for themselves. But they had to go along with their beast into the stable for shelter. Everything is in the hands of God, so they accept what he provides and later when the labor pains started, Joseph simply went down to the Inn asking for a woman's help and I am sure in that society there was always someone available. Too bad that the Scriptures do not mention her or their names but it was thought at that time to be a very casual business like getting a meal or cleaning the house and not a task worthy of immortality in such a monument that St. Luke put together. Joseph stood by, of course, waiting for the first cry of a baby born, completely lost in thought at the wonder of it all and trying to figure out his role in the days that were coming. Surely it was that of guardian as he found out in a hurry when the angel casually told him to get going all the way to Egypt as there were they who sought the life of the child-already a threat to so many. In the meantime he had to rustle up some turtle doves, welcome the shepherds as they came and pay proper host to the three men from the Orient—and no doubt be ravished by the singing of the angels as the melody rose and fell in the night sky. Good Joseph, for at least six months, ever since Mary returned from her visit to Elizabeth and he was told that the abstention he noted in his promised bride was the work of the Holy Spirit, he has been a man bewildered; one moment he is in ecstasy over the closeness of Israel God, the next beating his breast at his unworthiness of such a vocation. No doubt very often he went out into the carpenter's shop and took out his feelings sawing logs or hammering nails. Men are like that in roles that are a bit beyond them. I imagine Mary looked on him in her calm, accepting fashion with love over his God-fomented turmoil. He has proved an example to all of us. We too have a role thrust upon us precisely precisioned for our particular make-up. Let us ask Joseph to help us practice it as he did....

So we have got a little preaching in this morning. Even though you are not yet gone off but are still marking Ursuline time no doubt at Brown County. You will have a beautiful Christmas I know in the spiritual family there with all your friends....

God bless all. My love to each and everyone. And may you all be jolly and full of laughter as the joy of Christmas bubbles out of you. Merry Christmas. And much love.

Uncle Stanley

On Everlasting Rebellion and Overreaching Love

"Power at its best is love implementing the demands of justice. Justice at its best is love correcting everything that stands against love."
—Martin Luther King, Jr.

> "Beset by weakness...."
> —Hebrews 5:2

> "We sat down together and talked at length on the everlasting rebellion and weaknesses of man and the overreaching love of God: what might be called the ridiculous love affair that God carries on with his own, no matter how recalcitrant and unamiable they may be."
> —Uncle Stanley, letter 43

Dear One,

A power of evil is tearing our country apart again, still. Peace protests dissolve into violence. Rebellion trumps love. Revenge masquerades as justice. Unity feels illusive and impossible. Yet we go on: Hoping. Acting. Learning. Remembering. Staying at the table of dialogue. Sitting across from another. Confessing complicity.

    I wonder what is tearing you apart, stretching your resolve for peace, challenging your thinking? Whatever it might be, it may need to be held in stillness before action (or even giving it voice). Sitting across a table from another with a cup of tea sometimes helps. Or alone with one small candle lit against the darkness. Or on a front porch with open palms tenderly holding the fear, the anger, the confusion.

    Peace,

Ellen

    P.S. Watch for the coming of Love, as delicately as for the first star.

IN THE SEASON OF WINTER

....

Letter 43 from Dubuque, Iowa

My dear girl,

I am so very glad I came down here to make a Retreat. The atmosphere is just right, the accommodations more than adequate, the bucolic scene and smells as you approach the huge farm plant on your daily walks, afford a perfect background for prayer and meditation. Fr. Matthews of Dundee is with me. This is the beginning of the third day and we have just made our confessions. Father Joe has just left leaving us with a feeling of satisfaction that in as much as we have come this far, we can expect to slide gracefully into heaven without splinters.

Confession is a device that has not been fairly used in the Church. I myself have not set a great deal of store by it—let us say only when I got stuck in the mud. But when used as we used it today, it is a wonderful contrivance for peace of mind. We sat down together and talked at length on the everlasting rebellion and weaknesses of man and the over-reaching love of God: what might be called the ridiculous love affair that God carries on with his own, no matter how recalcitrant and unamiable they may be. How plaintive he can be: "Why I myself taught Ephraim to walk, I took them in my arms…I led them with leading strings of love…" And what a pursuer-all this time, all these seventy-two years!

When I was young instead of studying theology, I committed to memory, "The Hound of Heaven"—During this week whole passages have been coming back to me—

"Now of that long pursuit
Comes on at hand the bruit;
That Voice is round me like a blessing sea:…"

> Wherefore should any set thee love apart?
> Seeing none but I makes much of naught....
>
> Alack, thou knowest not
> How little worthy of love though art!
> Whom wilt thou find to love ignoble thee,
> Save me, save only me?...
>
> Halts by me that footfall:
> Is my gloom, after all,
> Shade of His hand, outstretched caressingly?"
> —From "The Hound of Heaven" by Francis Thompson

Father Joe gave the two of us a talk yesterday afternoon on old age and ultimate things. It was just what we needed to calm us both and to make us glad we came. We will go home tomorrow after lunch—367 miles! I must be ready to take Charles' place Friday morning as he leaves tomorrow for Ireland. For three weeks I shall bear the beats of the day and then seek some rest in Florida and/or Long Island. Already I have in my pocket a round-trip ticket presented by a loving Christian man....

8:25 PM
Still bright out with every detail of the landscape which from my room looks Italian, etched against the aftermath of a lingering sun. The door is now locked and presumably the monks are all in bed. They have been up since 3 AM. I have paragraphs (or written pages) to go before I sleep (or attempt to sleep at 10:30). I do not get up in the night for Matins. I get up at 6 AM and am in chapel for Lauds. At 7 AM we go into the enclosure and concelebrate with twenty to forty monks. The Office and the Mass are all in English and the hymns are Catholic, Protestant and many modern. It is a great high Mass done by the liturgical nines! This morning the chants and hymns were all accompanied by guitars and the choral ensemble simply buried you. I was enthralled!

I regret I do not have your letter here to comment on. It was a dandy letter and so much you in it that I longed to see you. (Somehow or other I manage to "read" you perfectly and I can mull over your letters like a lover because it is such a delight to see you grow.) I was delighted to talk to Carol. She sounded so alive! There will be so much to talk about as the nieces come home. I would love to listen but now as Thoreau said: "the first star is lit and I go home." [From the journal of Henry D. Thoreau]

God bless you,

Uncle Stanley

On Jubilee

> "When you are seventy-seven and about to celebrate
> your fiftieth there is little left to crow about. And I will
> bet you that if any foolish expositor of "This is Your Life"
> dares to get up on May 2 to extol the monumental
> works of Father Hale, he will concentrate on the brick
> and mortar that stand on every side and will
> not even conceive the far more important fact that he
> loved Ellen Doyle with all the love of his heart."
> —Uncle Stanley, letter 84

*D*ear One,

I would have celebrated fifty years since my first commitment this past year (as is the tradition in my community) but alas, the date got postponed because of the pandemic. Instead it will be held three years later, this time fifty years from final vows, perhaps a more fitting date after all. Hopefully,

Doyle Family: Bottom step: Sarah, second step: Barry, Amy, Joe, third step: Bonnie (Tim's wife), Ellen; fourth step: Jeanie, Uncle Stanley; top step: Mary Kay, Tim, Grandma Hale with Tim and Bonnie's baby Michael, Mom, Dad. St. Martin, Ohio, August 1973, Final Vows.

it can be held in my parish in the midst of families, friends, and the Sisters who remain among us. In any case, it will be a celebration, a day of gratitude, joy, blessing.

I have the invitation to my 1973 final vows on my kitchen wall with the cover quote from James Carroll, the same one I sent to Uncle Stanley for his jubilee: "This is clearly a moment of some other making than mine. You, O God, have graced me, gifted me, made me mute again with a spark of your vastness that is unwinding itself in my days of growing and threading itself into a future of absolute You, me, all my others, and song."

I may well use it again for my day of jubilee, trusting that there still will be days of growing to look forward to, and the continuation of my intention to be mute again (still) in the face of such vast love....

Ellen

P.S. I'm wondering about the jubilees in your circle of family and friends... Do you have someone you love who has celebrated a jubilee? Write about the celebration and what it meant to you to serve as a witness or perhaps as the one celebrating....

....

Letter 84 from Sun City, Arizona

Dear Ellen dear,

I sit out here on the green green grass at 2:03 PM hoping the sun will come out to shoot its sharpest rays at me as it is probably the final salvo before I take off early Monday morning. I am reluctant to go but I need to check in at my doctors, pay my end-of-the-month bills, make at least mental preparations for my fiftieth, May 2, and take up the communication slack with all my good friends. I hope spring has ventured North far enough to prevent an un-bleaching of my hide as a tan out-of-season is the only advantage I have over my fellow men. It is the only way that I could possibly arouse envy in the breast of another as my beauty has given way to ugliness, my mind to senility, my vigor to decrepitude. When you are seventy-seven and about to celebrate your fiftieth there is little left to crow about. And I will bet you that if any foolish expositor of "This is Your Life" dares to get up on May 2 to extol the monumental works of Father Hale, he will concentrate on the brick and mortar that stand on every side and will not even conceive the far more important fact that he loved Ellen Doyle with all the love of his heart. So little do men know about their contemporaries. Your letter wilted me is they all do. I nervously ask with....

Friday
*D*ear Ellen dear,

The sun pours into my morning window and I sit here like a stranger at this machine that has not been caressed by my fingers for two months. I just know that I will mess up this sheet of paper with all kinds of odd characters and vowels in consonantal places and vice versa. In Sun City I had recourse to printing which is almost a complete reversion to childhood because my handwriting has deteriorated so. It never was very much and always looked as if a thousand hens had walked across the paper after spending the night in a mud puddle. I know all I have to do is to give you a glimmer of my thought in even hieroglyphs and your love would take it from there. Speaking of love I enclose a sheet or two I wrote in Sun City and never got back to. No use wasting it as ideas are expensive and my parsimony of ideas is such that I can't afford to throw them away....

I have been back for almost two weeks and the weather has been delightful every day. Not as warm as Arizona but sunny. I was welcomed back with open arms and it feels so good to be accepted and appreciated. Genuinely, I mean, and not perfunctorily and one can tell the difference. But I must say that my stay in Arizona was a love experience. Pat and I felt very close and did each other a lot of good. She deplored that she couldn't get up to the Fiftieth as Julia would be the only sibling present. But in a letter yesterday she said that she is determined to come if only for twenty-four hours....

Your letter to Arizona made my stay. Just think of being way out there in the desert feeling like a prickly cactus and looking like an ancient saguaro that is supposed to produce an arm every two-hundred years and know all the time that you are in somebody's thought and that she is sending messages to you in spirit! Such thoughts, such messages stir me deeply and cause me to swoon with delight but they don't compare with a letter in the mail! But of course I cannot expect you to do better than you do as you are the busiest and also when you do produce you are the bestest.

...The four walls here were telling me yesterday that they are lonesome and would like to enfold you; my frying pan is just dying to fry an egg just for you, my big window pane is full of pain because you haven't been here to look through it, my easy chair is simply falling apart because as she said, you have been ignoring her; the downright loneliness of this house for need of you is getting on my nerves, I bring all these things to your attention just to let you know how much matter agonizes over your absence. The spiritual is much worse off. I wake up in the night and the angel of the house is not at peace. I hear wings restless in the dark and your name bemoaned. I try to pray and I am distracted by what I think is the rustle of your presence. (Skirts don't rustle anymore or do they?) I try to say Mass and you walk in and grab off all my intentions. So you can see that far better your presence than all this furor of your absence....

...Your transports of love for God set me winging too and I identify with you as you take off on your flight of exaltation. I plunge deeply into Holy Week, walk steadily with His mother, suffer the agony and ecstasy of Magdalen, cry with Peter, walk down to Emmaus and hurry back to Jerusalem (New) and spread the good news. I love you very much.

Uncle Stanley

On Wills, Bequests and Other Treasures

"I shall mark the Shamrock cup—that it returns to you.
Would you like for me to return all your letters to me?
If so I must put them in order and have an orgy
of rereading before I do."
—Uncle Stanley, letter 125

> "For a divine seed, the crown of destiny,
> Is hidden and sown on an ancient, fertile plain
> You hold the title to."
>
> —From "In a Tree House," by Hafiz

*D*ear One,

During these days and weeks and months of a world-wide pandemic, people are making wills: People who may not have thought of it until a real threat emerged or who think of themselves as too young, as not yet ready to ponder such life-and-death matters.

Several decades ago my community mandated that each of us update our wills. I complied, having little to claim and no direct descendants to consider. But Sr. Imelda, the oldest in our community at the time, nearing ninety, was resistant. She did not see the point. One day, as she paced back and forth in the hall outside my room, complaining about receiving yet another reminder and another copy of the form to complete, I posed the possibility: "You could will me your garden, you know!" I piqued her interest! "Yes," I said, "you could make known your wishes right here on the form for your will."

At that point, Sr. Imelda, all of five feet tall, had spent probably thirty years since her retirement from teaching creating her private garden. She had built hedges and sheds, planted rose bushes and Jewels-of-Tibet, weeded and tilled that very secret garden. Despite her meager efforts at securing it from unwanted visitors like young campers and surreptitious students, it was possible to earn a spontaneous invitation to visit but only on her terms. From my office at Chatfield College, I could see her comings and goings, watch her unlock the rickety gate, pass through the narrow opening in the twenty-foot tall hedge, and reappear at the end of day in her sweaty bonnet, dirty habit and muddy boots, just in time for Vespers.

Sr. Imelda did will her garden to me, knowing I appreciated it. My tiny plot of herbs behind one of our college buildings was a miniature field for my own gardening efforts, knowing I did not have the time then to really invest in its fertility. Several years later, I received a call from the person-in-charge asking if I wanted any of Sr. Imelda's garden tools. My long service at Chatfield had ended, I had moved and a new ministry involved extensive travel with no time for serious gardening beyond another tiny herb garden, fifteen miles away from my original one. Sr. Imelda had died and her garden was going to be uprooted and tilled under to make room for a new building. I claimed her watering can and a few tools, now well over seventy-five years old. I use them still. And during this pandemic since all travel has been postponed, there is the time I've never had to till and plant and harvest.

Last week, I mailed my grand-niece Millie a book called *Babies*, by Gyo Fujikawa. It is one of those hard-paged books that babies love to play with long before they can read. It has pictures of lots of babies doing all kinds of things. It begins and ends with the mantra: "Babies are very very soft, warm and cuddly…" Millie is now four-years-old and along with her delighted parents is awaiting the birth of twin baby brothers later this year. Knowing Millie had hoped for at least one baby sister, I decided she needed cheering up. The book called *Babies* is charming, with a four-year-old boy pictured on the cover reading the *Babies* book to his new baby sister. Millie's grandpa, my youngest brother Joe, was about four when the *Babies* book was published in 1963, just in time for the birth of our youngest baby sister Amy (who I just learned has the whole book memorized). So I bought a new copy of the book (still in print) and wrote Millie a hand-written letter about her Grandpa Joe reading this book to our little sister Amy when he was four. I encouraged her to learn to read it before her little brothers arrive. Her mother and grandpa reported tears after reading my letter, loving the gift which created a new memory to be passed on to a new generation.

Uncle Stanley gave me several books from his extensive library before he died. But the two that mean the most to me are the two we read together, out loud, in his Worthington, Minnesota, living room after he retired: *Through the Looking Glass* and *The Hunting of the Snark*, both by Lewis Carroll and published in England in 1871 and 1876 respectively. I have the miniature versions of each, bound in dull red linen with gold-embossed images of the Red (or is it the White?) Queen and the determined Bellman on the two covers. Those versions were both published in 1908 and 1910, reprinted in London for the fifth or eleventh time in the early 1920s, purchased as a pair by Uncle Stanley in Rome in 1923 (when he was twenty-four), and snail-mailed to me in Ohio in 1980 (when I was thirty-one). They are among my most valuable treasures.

But I have not yet decided what to do with them after I am gone. I must get on that. And find someone to read them to, out loud, probably in North Carolina where most of my nieces, nephews and grands live. And give them away while I can still laugh and cry over the words, the stories, and the pictures with someone I love. After all, like Sr. Imelda protested, wills are really pointless in the end. It's the collection of stories that we live through along the way that is our true treasure.

Hoping you are well, safe from any pandemic that might be threatening, and living fully your own stories.

Love to you, dear,

Ellen

P.S. Is there something you own that you treasure so much that you might give it away someday to someone very dear to you or put it in your will? Write a story about it…and give it to someone you love.

....

Letter 125 from Caledonia, Minnesota

Monday evening
My dear Ellen,

It is early in the evening as you can see but it is already pitch dark outside with the time change and I have just come in from saying my rosary. I have been walking up and down reveling in the lovely warm Indian Summer weather that we have been having and thanking God for all his goodness. I came over here on Friday in time for a grandparents and grandchildren Mass and program and luncheon. Every person had to have a grandparent except the grandparents....

This afternoon Charlie and I took off to get lost in the hills and valleys of Houston County and to enjoy the remnants of the fall foliage where it might appear in sumac or in a belated maple reluctant to go naked the rest of the winter. It was a beautiful drive and ended up close to the river so we decided to go into La Crosse for a big dish of ice cream. Afterwards he stopped at the Hospital to see what there was to be seen around the crib of a two-year-old dying of cancer of the brain...

I wrote a letter to your mother this morning as she had one coming and I was in a mood to tell her I love her. Maybe I can get at least one letter written each day I am here. I expect to leave on Thursday, All Souls, and gradually crawl back to Worthington. I'll have my own car and it is a long way and I shall go slowly, maybe stopping in to take Julia out to dinner and staying the night. The weather is supposed to stay put until the week-end. Of course I don't trust November weather. Too many goblins, leprechauns and things that go bump in the night, to say nothing, of ice, blizzards, sleet and rains.

Your last letter was simply beautiful and your special quality was alive in every sentence. You said that you wished for more hours and days to get what you had to say in better words. An impossible wish, an absurd hope. Had you meditated from now to Christmas you could have done no better. The setting, with back-ground music (which I can never stand when I am trying to read or write) and the murmur of sisters, helped to open you up and pour forth your heart....

I shall mark the Shamrock cup—that it returns to you. [This was my gift to him for his jubilee, now sitting on my Grandmother's desk in my living room.] Would you like for me to return all your letters to me? If so I must put them in order and have an orgy of rereading before I do. I don't remember throwing any of them away. They are the history of your soul in a way and certainly of your growth in the Lord. But also the story of your developing love for me that started in my house with your eager interested eyes burning a hole in my heart. That is the day you ceased to be a mere niece and became a lover. And that love has been the light of my old age and the delight of my days. I thank God for you constantly as the thought of you pulls me out of every dull or melancholy orbit. I need only say that Ellen loves me to carry on and on. Thank you, my love.

God love you now. I see I didn't say one word about the Retreat which was just what I needed. But I have copious notes and will take it up another day. I love you too.

Your Uncle Stanislaus (the John Paul II influence)!

Uncle Stanley

On Waiting

> "You are so dear to me that if anything should happen to you I think the leaves would fall from the day and total darkness would envelop my world. I have another friend: Marylyn Adel, whom you met here and lives across the street from the Rectory. I just sit waiting for further word from Minneapolis as to whether she is to live or die."
> —Uncle Stanley, letter 152

> "While I wait I am waiting for strawberries to freeze one by one...."
> —Uncle Stanley, letter 152

> "I save it until the precise moment comes when
> I can drink it in, pour over it, spend time on it
> and love it the way it deserves."
> —Uncle Stanley, letter 152

> "Strange how hunger can dominate desire."
> —Uncle Stanley, letter 152

Dear Ones,

My good friend Mike Fullam died this morning. And my spirit is in that liminal time and space of waiting and wondering. Wondering about the mystery of his life now in communion with the God who was his first love. Wondering about the joy of his reuniting with his wife Kate, gone two years now as Mike waited for his own time. Wondering if I will be able to go to his Philadelphia funeral and meet face-to-face and heart-to-heart with his sister Colleen, his son Daniel, his granddaughter Sloane Maureen and the others in their very Irish clan. And so I wonder and wait....

When I was a kid, I figured out a way to make my Halloween candy last until Easter. It drove my siblings crazy. And no doubt is an indication of being a little obsessive compulsive! It shifted the waiting from a bi-yearly special event to a daily one.

Now I no longer measure out treats to shorten the waiting time. I no longer count weeks and days and minutes. Instead I am more inclined to watch and wait, relishing the present moment. Waiting, without knowing the day or the hour, has its own grace. Unless, of course, that the waiting is filled with fear about a diagnosis, a decision to be made, word about the wellbeing of someone lost or estranged. In that case, entrusting the waiting to others lightens the worry.

I am wondering what you wait for, watch for, wonder or worry about at this stage in your life... Whatever, may there be joy (or maybe peace or someone to hold it with you) along the way....

Peace,

Ellen

P.S. Write about a worry. Or something you are waiting for, longing for, wondering about.

....

Letter 152 from Worthington, Minnesota

My dear Ellen,

When I say my dear Ellen you know that I am conveying a dearness that is beyond speech or a superscription to convey. You are so dear to me that if anything should happen to you I think the leaves would fall from the day and total darkness would envelop my world. I have another friend: Marylyn Adel, whom you met here and lives across the street from the Rectory. I just sit waiting for further word from Minneapolis as to whether she is to live or die. For five weeks she was down with MS, violent headaches, nausea and double vision. Finally they took her to an expert in Minneapolis who discovered no MS but a brain tumor which when operated on turned out to be malignant. They seem to have got it all and she made an excellent recovery for three days when night before last she went into a decline that has us all on the ropes. Papa summoned all the children yesterday morning so I don't know what is going on. Imagine the prayers that have been said by many for that bright and shining girl who has given such joy and happiness to so many.

While I wait I am waiting for strawberries to freeze one by one on a cooking-sheet so I can put them into a bag. A half dozen people were picking them this morning, stopped in with five pounds and stayed for Mass. So I have been busy washing them and getting them frozen. I am piling them up for the future, for next winter no less when maybe I won't be around to eat them. But then somebody will. Should you come along later in the summer I could fill you up on them. Which reminds me of your mother's invitation to meet the family in Cincy at the end of August or thereabouts. As of now I would not presume to venture but then at that time it may be feasible. But I don't mind telling you that I think my travelling days are over. My breathing becomes more labored and humidity is a serious problem as you know. Just now I am so well content to be at home that I could purr. The week before last I went down to the ordinations in Winona and stayed with Charles in Eyota for a week. It went off well enough as the weather was cool. But I was glad to come home on the bus on Saturday. Then last Monday I drove up to Mankato and picked up Julia who stayed with me all, week and left Saturday evening. That night I had a mind to call you on Sunday night but decided I would wait for the letter that was bound to come the next day. And there it was!!! It was a lovely letter as all your letters are. At times I pick them out of my desk where they piled and read one and it is as if I had a good visit with you. Letter visits are more heart-warming anyway than phone calls. I was never very efficient on a phone. After the call is over I generally beat myself into insensibility because I didn't remember to say this or that. But just to hear your voice is very heaven.

 It is humbling to realize that you treat my poor letters just like I treat yours. My mail comes after lunch which is no time to savor a letter from you. So I save it until the precise moment comes when I can drink it in, pour over it, spend time on it and love it the way it deserves. This time that great apostrophe of yours to God working in the lives of all whom we mention, whom we love, who make up our lives was the best you have ever done and completely beyond me to equal. I have gone over it and over it and each time come away exalted and in a mood to hug the Lord for giving me you for a friend and for putting a pen in your hand. The very nub of it deserves a kiss and preservation in the Hall of Pens along with John Hancock's feather.

 …It is now Thursday and the pastor has called to invite me to the lake this afternoon to honor a priest who is leaving for another parish.

I accepted with Joy. Also he got word that Marylyn was conscious yesterday but they have found a new lump on her breast. Poor child! Also I was able to tell him that I anointed one of his parishioners last night as he was not about—the very first time in seven years. Pretty good, we both thought!

I would feign hang on but it is time for lunch and I feel gentle gnawings in my innards. Strange how hunger can dominate desire. So God bless you dearly. I love you dearly and I am sure the whole world loves you dearly.

Always your

Uncle Stanley

On Winter

"Every convent, I think, has a green thumb somewhere in its thumb-shed which begins to twitch as winter grudgingly lets go of the good earth and the worms begin their probing towards the daylight."
—Uncle Stanley, letter 7

"I must say that I am happy that the Christmastide has slipped away into the frost kilns of old man Boreas. Tonight the world is heaven with every tree coated with frost and the snow about three feet on the level and as white as the angel (any angel) with the guitar. It is sheer magic."
—Uncle Stanley, letter 29

IN THE SEASON OF WINTER

> "Please God I will be going home on the sixteenth. There is still six feet of snow everywhere and I hope I don't land in the same drift I managed to extricate myself from in January. But I certainly will be able to take it better as the apple blossoms will be burgeoning forth, the tulips popping their noses out of the ground, the robin's nests ready to take wing and maybe a spear of green grass."
> —Uncle Stanley, letter 193

Dear One,

Yesterday's weather report alerted me to the prediction that last night was to have been the coldest it's been since April. By the crunchy feel of the crisp grass beneath my slippered-feet when I retrieved the newspaper this morning, they were right. But I still rather like winter. Its propelling wind and early darkness turns me inward toward cozier clothes, peasant soups, candles burning in each room and good long books.

I remember that once Uncle Stanley retired at least one letter each year was filled with his own propelling desire to retreat from the fury of the Minnesota winter to be enveloped by his sister Pat's hospitality in Phoenix. [Patricia Schaefer was J. Stanley Hale's youngest sister and had retired to Arizona where she lived alone after her husband died. She and Uncle Stanley were soul mates as well.] "My bones work again and my lungs too!" he shouted. He delighted in walking, breathing and reading outside on one sunny day after another. His heart and soul were invigorated by his sister's love. He always reclaimed his young self and brought it back in time for Holy Week and Easter in Minnesota.

Now I turn toward my own winter haven. The hour we gained when daylight savings gave way to ordinary time two weeks ago has slipped quietly into the darkness, leaving us still with just twenty-four hours each day. It hardly seems enough. Yet, I draw on my sabbatical learnings and a card that I still use as a mantra: There is plenty of time and each moment counts.

Warmly,

Ellen

P.S. I wonder what YOU do when the climate is unfavorable? Paint a picture of that scene, that season, that safe haven. Or write a poem....

....

Letter 7 from Worthington, Minnesota

My dear Ellen,

Easter looms up at the end of the week like a big sign on an interstate highway telling the wonders of vacationland. It is the Way, the Hope, the Sign of Jonah, the Prophet. It is the end of penance, the receptacle for the ashes, the angels' skyway, the pastor's goal, the associates release: "I'll go home and visit the folks; I'll be back Wednesday." The thrust that started so casually and slowly on the first Sunday of Advent, began to move at Christmas and got into high gear only on Septuagesima, full throttle during Passiontide, reaches its apogee on this day of days. Throats grow raw on Alleluias, trying to out Cherubim the Seraphim. From this day the liturgy runs downhill coming almost to a full stop on the strained analogies on the thirteenth Sunday. In the meantime, spring comes to the land, with summer hot on its trail. Young men go forth to war, old men seek the comfort of the shade trees and young novices wonder about their habits. Not their virtues or their vices, habits both, but their habiliments to see whether Dacron is to be worn this year or linen and wool. Strange how we must cling to the medieval dry goods when even salvation itself has gone modern and life everlasting can be obtained by means undreamed of by a man like Francis who could walk the street in old brown wadmal and nothing in his wallet whereas a contemporary savior of the world in mod clothes paints a sign and pickets the chancery demanding that the rich Church should give its all to the cause of the poor. And then steps into his Mustang and whizzes away with the subdued roar of his exhaust to the happening at the Tavern on the Green. There he will whisk out his guitar and soulfully sing the antiphon to "Gotta love my sister, gotta love my brother, gotta love the Lord." And Ronnie Welsch, the ex-priest, will line up the parade to March up Plymouth Avenue in Minneapolis in honor of Martin Luther King, bless him, while all his contemporary priests will be offering up a Mass for Martin's soul. [Martin Luther King was assassinated on April 4, 1968.] And he will have the wonderful satisfaction of being "with-it" all the way. And life will be wonderfully meaningful and relevant. And full of beer.

Your grandmother I had met with on Monday in Madelia and she will be here on Easter Sunday with the Quinns, assorted Quinns, including all hereabouts. The weather is perfect, has been for over two months. The sun pours out its rays every day like a lamp in the sanctuary—non-stop. It does not rain enough. That is why we pray to the Lord every day to send rain to the thirsty land. The buds are bursting forth and the voice of the turtle may be heard. Only one of the unpleasant things about becoming deaf is that one cannot hear it. And I always loved its tranquil note, its melancholy sound. Like a bass saxophone. When I was in Ellsworth years ago it was the sound of a summer morning and the key note of Matins as I walked up and down flinging verses right and left and convincing the people that the pastor was nuts.

Lent has been a grand experience. I did not mind it at all but gloried in its nuances. The people came out to Mass in the morning and afternoon in serried ranks. Words of wisdom sprang from the lips of the homilist like honey flowing from a pancake flask and just as sweet!

Every convent, I think, has a green thumb somewhere in its thumb-shed which begins to twitch as winter grudgingly lets go of the good earth and the worms begin their probing towards the daylight. Sister Mary Thumb, they call her and she usually is wrinkled and old and sweet and beautiful like the flowers that respond to her charismatic finger. So in your community her name is Anthony. That is a good name for her. Haunched over her flower beds she can think about her patron all day long—his learning (he is a Doctor of the Church), his gentleness (the doves coddled him), his sanctity (he could work and odd miracle), and his truly remarkable memory (he can remember where people left things). So if seeds fall through little holes in her pack or names escape through little holes in her mind, she can just say: "Tony, get busy!" (This, you can see, is a digression.)

I did not hear about the family portrait [see photo on page 21] but it must be okay since you are younger than Mary Kay. What does she wear that makes her look so much older, a moustache? And Joey growing like Jack and the Beanstalk before our very eyes. He should suppress his yen for size and heed the Lord, who said: "And who, by taking thought, can add to his stature one cubit?" Would you like to have a cubit sitting on top of your head? (Excuse it, please.)

Dr. Joe Schaefer left for Moscow this morning. Now who would want to go to Moscow except a man who would like to say: "I've been to Moscow." His wife, Patricia, has chosen the better part; she will go to Ireland and Rome. Now who wouldn't like to go to Ireland and Rome? Every last Ursuline in St. Ursula's quiver, I'd say....

Do have a beautiful Easter. Does the family get up there on that day? If not, you may open this letter and read it. A melancholy substitute, I know, but the beggars of the Lord cannot be choosers. I would like to close with a verse from the Passiontide Terce. It's a bombshell and I don't know what it means:

May the Lord save you from the lion's mouth,
And from the horns of the wild bulls.

Your

Uncle Stanley

IN THE SEASON OF WINTER

....

Letter 29 from Worthington, Minnesota

My dear Ellen Doyle,

I have reached the end of my rope. I can't sleep. I can't drink, smoke, or talk to girls. I have three letters in a row from you, short of course, but authentic scribblings duly signed and full of parts of speech, idioms, misspellings, diacritical marks, grammar and punctuation. I am red in the face, in a blue funk, discolored with black misgivings. I got up this morning ·with only one thought in mind and that was to write a letter to my favorite niece. It is now close to 9 PM. and I have just stuck the sheet in the machine. In the meantime I have had one hassle after another as they (the hassles, I mean) were all piled up for my sins during the past three days while I was gone from the parish....

I must say that I am happy that the Christmastide has slipped away into the frost kilns of old man Boreas. Tonight the world is heaven with every tree coated with frost and the snow about three feet on the level and as white as the angel (any angel) with the guitar. It is sheer magic. And never have we had such a magical winter with great quantities of snow everywhere but all lying peacefully on the land like a benediction. No violence of wind, no scud of rain, no layers of dust have marred the surfaces of the earth. Just snow. Last year we had a blizzard every day with a wind that violated the snow until it was scourged to a series of pillars that looked tall on the plains and left one hating the day and the place of one's birth. What a contrast! In some places like Minneapolis it has snowed five days in succession without a let up. But it was so gentle, so benign, so purifying that nobody minded it, and it moved the people to buy just more and more snowmobiles. There are thousand about. A winter Wonderland!

Aw g'wan, sez you! He is just trying to make not only a virtue out of necessity but a prose poem out of a bunch of icicles. Not so, sez he. He states it as it is. But at the same time he can't believe he is the same person who cursed every flake last year and in disgust crawled on his hands and knees all the way to freedom and the open road to California. It is the Wind that moaneth bleak! Right, it is the Wind that makes the difference.

I did not hear either how things went off re Wilmington. I hope that it is an enterprise that will please them all and help all and sanctify all. It will leave you about half way between Worthington and Wilmington so that on your days off you will have to choose between the W's—like Volkswagen. But it would be a fine thing for an Ursuline to come to the land of the big black Ursas and be comforted and renewed by such tinkling sounds as Minnehaha or the never never cry of the loon—one of nature's finest sounds. I dare to say that Nell will not be along for some time yet, maybe not until the spring thaw. But maybe by this time she is homesick for bridge and gossip and tea and an occasional glimpse of her own rooftree. Maybe she just awaits the outcome of the negotiations now pending. Maybe she is waiting for Godot. Who and what does an old lady wait for when the parade has all gone by? I have an inkle I know... But could it be heaven?

Friday morning.
A bird interfered with my stance last night and I never did get back to this machine. I now resume at precisely 11:06 AM. The "boys" have gone out snowmobiling. Parishioners loan them the machines. I am an advocate of skiing where one needs some skill and energy but this snowmobiling seems terribly childish. One doesn't go anywhere except in circles and INSIDE the fences. Like a bull on roller skates. Anything with a motor in it, even a broom is grist to their mill. But nothing that will take energy. Ah me! But as I was saying Friday is their day off so I run the place alone, I try to get all middling things (like this) off in the morning and in the afternoon, I go and call on the nursing homes. In the evening I start putting together the Sunday Bulletin. In between times I eat, drink, read, answer phones and drink and eat. So and in this fashion an ordinary Friday slips into history—without a single thing to record for posterity…

It is time for lunch and I must go. I could leave this in the typewriter with the hope that something would turn up that would pique your interest but then again I may forget to get it mailed today. And I think it is high time to get something down to St. Martin's if only a post card.

My love to all the nieces and a special big love for you
Thine,

Uncle Stanley

....

Letter 193 from Sun City, Arizona

My dear Ellen,

It isn't that I have been browned nicely on all sides nor that I have forgotten you but time has slipped by so fast with every single day precisely the same as the day before. Not a drop of rain, nothing but sun and the moon in the sky, so close you could touch it. And energy to burn—a commodity that I thought I had lost before I came out here. But I have been busy as a bee, happy, healthy, sassy and full of beans....

This morning's paper tells of great tornadoes in the Carolinas. I hope they missed Wrightsville Beach as that seems to be exposed and quite vulnerable should a tornado come along. No doubt your mama and Barry's wife Denise will be preparing to visit Cincy for the Retreat. No doubt you will see them there. It will be a grand visit. Also you will see Mary and Ceil, God bless her. And you will be rooting around, looking for some chink in the wall that will disclose what you will do next year. Since you closed the door in Chicago I hope something else has opened up waiting for you to walk in. Your St. Patrick's Day card was not very definite as to what.

Please God I will be going home on the sixteenth. There is still six feet of snow everywhere and I hope I don't land in the same drift I managed to extricate myself from in January. But I certainly will be able to take it better as the apple blossoms will be burgeoning forth, the tulips popping their noses out of the ground, the robin's nests ready to take wing and maybe a spear of green grass. Here the flowers are already rioting and spring has burst out all over. But apart from the flowers the only real difference from winter is the thermometer which has gone from seventy to eighty. You can imagine me blithely taking to the road in the afternoons sniffing the ozone, breathing deep and fingering the sorrowful mysteries. I move along like a deep contemplative but actually have a hard time to keep my mind on what I am doing. I can go through the whole scourging at the pillar between one sniff and another...

But speaking of the scourging I have been reading the Report on the Shroud of Turin by Dr. John Heller. It is the report of the forty scientists who examined the Shroud in 1978. It is one of the most fascinating books I have ever read in spite of the scientific jargon and makes monkeys out of would-be interpreters who try to say it is a painting. It is blood. Whose blood, they do not say. But what that man went through is precisely what the Gospel says Jesus of Nazareth went through. Since they never met Jesus of Nazareth, know not his blood type, nor the date of the cloth (as yet), they didn't venture to put a name to it. And how it affected the scientists involved it does not say except Heller, a Southern Baptist from Yale, says at the end that he has moved out of the Acropolis and a little closer to Jerusalem. You would love it....

It is time for Mass... Have a Happy Easter although I will be on the phone after I get home. God bless and I love you dearly.

Uncle Stanley

IN THE SEASON OF WINTER

On Last Things

THE LAST THREE LETTERS

Letter 198 from Sun City, Arizona

My dear Ellen,

First of all let me warn you against this machine. It may take off and jump right in your eye. I will try to control it with what strength I have but it has me defeated. I rented it yesterday way over in Glenview as I need one badly because I am working on a correction (final) and revision of the Parish history. I need a nice clean copy to present to the printers and here this mad-hatter is ruining my peace of mind. The space control is completely out of whack.

Now that that is said I must tell you that I came out here a week ago today. I had a ticket for the week before that but went to the hospital instead with a slight case of pneumonia. After five days they thought me well enough to venture out. I had an excellent trip and was picked up at the airport by Pat Schaefer and Bette Cashman. The sun was blazing and it was close to seventy degrees. It has been glorious ever since. The Saturday after I left it was twenty-nine in Worthington and a wind chill of 90 degrees below zero. Am I glad I leaped!

Before I came I tried to get you on the phone several times but never succeeded so was happy to get your letter yesterday. You seem to be gadding about and worrying about many serious affairs. I hope all your prayers are answered and that the Lord carry you in the palm of his hand right to the very station where you are meant to work. With all your present training there must be many opportunities awaiting you. In the meantime you wait on the Lord.

...The Lord is certainly letting people know that he is the master of the weather as well as sea and sky to say nothing of the Order of St. Ursula.

The Scotch is aging in its ancient keg waiting for my tap on the barrel. After all one doesn't get to be eighty-six every day or even every lifetime. [Uncle Stanley's eighty-sixth and last birthday was January 26, 1985.] We plan to go forth and dine in semielegance....

I shall pray hard for the success of your elections for a new Council and that the best person wins. I shall say a Mass on March 2, please God. In the meantime keep me informed of any changes. as you know I love you.

Uncle Stanley

Uncle Stanley, St. Mary Church History, Worthington, Minnesota.

....

Letter 199 from Sun City, Arizona

My dear Ellen,

No doubt you are back in Chicago after the great election in St. Martin. I have been very anxious to find out whom you elected. I called there Saturday night but could not hear a word and told the operator to give you and Ceil my love. She tried to tell me who was chosen but I couldn't grasp it. I should have waited for Pat to come in and take over. I thought I might hear from you yesterday but I can see my anxiety moves me to try to annihilate space as it takes several days for mail to come from thence. Anyway I wanted to write you a letter to convey to you my love and my prayers on your behalf that you will land precisely where you were meant to land. With a new election a whole new keg of nails could be broached and I am anxious to hear.

Time is certainly rushing by and there are only a few weeks to go by before I fly out of here on April 1. Social life is picking up and this week has been somewhat strenuous. I hope the week-end will be quiet after another dinner tonight at the Country Club and a pair coming in tomorrow for Mass and luncheon. On Monday the Dugans, old friends of mine from Long Island were here and we had a delightful visit.

I really got things done since I came here. I went over the whole history with a meticulous eye, rewrote several paragraphs and finished two last chapters. I sent it off last week with great joy to my friend AND SCHOLAR, Janice O'Malley, to be fine-tooth combed. You can imagine with what a spirit of liberation I have faced the dawn ever since. I have been trying to catch up on my letter writing but that is a labor of love and a joy to do. I go about that as the best part of my day and pound away between ten in the morning and one when we eat lunch. It is now 12:40. Afterwards I will saunter over to the library to browse a bit and about three-thirty stop in a pub for a Bud Lite where I work my daily crossword puzzle. I get in a mile or a mile and a half enroute which is just about all I can take this year. Last year I would go that far and return but I limit myself to the breathing demanded. After dinner we play two games of gin-rummy and then I read office, say prayers, and whatever else I have on hand. Just now I am reading *That Strange Divine Sea: Reflections on Being a Catholic* by Christopher Derrick. It is a gem of a book on his own love for the Church. A delightful writer—who wrote the definitive life of C.S. Lewis, his friend. I read and reread—a necessity in old age, it seems.

Pat and I have concocted a scheme to do honor to Sister Julia on her ninetieth birthday. We have composed a letter which we are sending to all the nieces and nephews. (You are no immediate niece but I'll send you one so you will know what is going on. It may so happen that you could be present.) She is getting quite frail and we have limited the reception to two hours and one half on Sunday afternoon, April 28th. We are leaving it to the nieces and nephews to invite their own families.

I have been in great form since I came out here. I was a bit fearful of coming but everything has gone beautifully and I am very grateful to the Lord for all his blessing. In the desert I do find it hard to make a Lent. Of course I can give up chewing tobacco or change to Bourbon instead of Scotch or saying my beads but everything seems to be lacking in fervor. Maybe you could think of something I could do?

I hear rattlings in the kitchen so lunch will be on in a minute and I must take my pills—the without-which-nots of an eighty-six-year-old.

God bless now and Much love.

P. S. I did say the Mass for the Ursulines last Saturday and wrote a note to Ceil.

....

Letter 200, the last one, to me and all the nieces and nephews. Fitting, I think, that Uncle Stanley's last letter to me would be a public one.

𝒟ear Ellen,

We have a sister whom we wish to honor. Sister Mary Julia will be ninety years of age on April 18th. It is the custom among the Sisters of Notre Dame when a Sister reaches ninety to celebrate Mass in the main chapel and have a birthday cake and reception in the afternoon. To this reception close friends and relatives are invited.

Aware that few of us could be present on April 18th, which comes on a Thursday we have asked the Sisters whether we could celebrate this extraordinary event on Sunday, April 28th. They fully acquiesced. We thought a Mass, concelebrated by Fr. Charles and myself at 2:00 PM followed by a reception at which a birthday cake and coffee would be served would be in order. Due to the present frailty of Sister Julia we thought a two and one-half hour session over-all, would be about right.

This would mean that all who came would be on their own for lunch and dinner. There would be no reason why we can't make this a family reunion and dine together, for instance, at the Country Pub near St. Peter; or at the Holiday at Kasota if someone of us has access to it.

You may be sure that we have more in mind than a reception for Sister Julia. We are intensely aware how beholden every single one of us is to her over the years. Her prayer-power, as you know, is terrific and unceasingly as she prayed for us through all the crises that beset us over the years. They still go on touching you and you and you.

Thus we would like to give her an ample gift that she could bestow on her Order if she so wills. In all her life she has never been able to contribute to her beloved community anything in the way of gifts or legacy. Many Wills have been made out as time has gone on and not once was she ever mentioned. It is time for the family to do something. We have thought that a thousand dollars or more would at least be a token. Lest you faint we will say that from a few in the know already $600.00 has been gathered. The givers insist that no name nor amount be mentioned nor will your name or amount be mentioned should you care to add to the sum above.

No matter whether you give or not we do beg you to be present for the event by two o'clock on Sunday afternoon, April 28th. It will be necessary for the Sisters to know how many will be present beforehand. Thus we ask that you send notice together with your check, should you so mind, to Worthington by April 21st.

God bless all and much love to all.
Father Stanley and Patricia L. Schaefer

We are sending this only to Sister Julia's nieces and nephews. You are asked to invite the members of your own families. Please let us know how many will be present by April 21st.

J.S. H.P.S.

Epilogue

The above mandala, with its tagline: *Holding the Center, Stretching Possibilities*, is Ellen Doyle's logo for her work in the world and serves as her email signature. Its inward and outward movements both keep her focused on what is hers to do in the present and open to what is needed in the wider community going forward.

After receiving a dire diagnosis of metastasized cancer on April 19, 2023, despite no pain or symptoms, Ellen heard from many loved ones and colleagues as news of her cancer spread about how timely and relevant her logo and tagline are. As this book goes to print, *Holding the Center* of what (and who) is most important in Ellen's life and *Stretching* beyond even 11 unimaginable *Possibilities* God has in store for her seems to matter most. Like that unreachable star in The Man of La Mancha's *Impossible Dream,* some invisible wisdom is guiding her, keeping her open to the new intergenerational relationships that are emerging and grateful for the gift of every season of her life!

You, as part of Ellen's community of readers (look for yourself in the circle of 11 people holding hands in the mandala), are also invited to *Hold the Center, Stretch Possibilities* in your own life and intergenerational relationships no matter what season you are living!

*D*earest One,

This is my last letter. And it is bittersweet. This journey with you, with Uncle Stanley, with these musings about life is coming to an end.

In recent years my five closest friends have died. Some of their words, a few of their gifts, and all of their love remains in my heart. In anticipation of moving to a smaller place, I cleaned out all of my closets and storage places, reducing my "things" by a third. And also recently, my Ursuline community has settled many of our last things as we come to completion. Although we no longer own any property, we still meet monthly and have one another, our stories and our love for one another. All this has been and still is bittersweet.

Yet strangely, releasing last things can be freeing, purifying... A sifting through memories, keepsakes, and relationships can lead to a delicate clarity, to the heart of the matter, even to an intimacy unattached to places, objects or time.

Uncle Stanley and I spent many hours on the phone between his last personal letter (#199), dated March 7, 1985, and his death in August 1985. Those words are gone. I did not even write in my journal during that period. And his last known letter was written not to me but to dear Cecilia, now also gone from among us (see p. 107).

My last visit with Uncle Stanley was the weekend of April 28, 1985, at his sister, Sister Julia's, ninetieth birthday gathering in Mankato, Minnesota. It was the last time I would see him in this life. Ironically, that last day with Uncle Stanley would have been his brother's, my grandfather's, eighty-eighth birthday. It was Grandpa's decision to marry my grandmother Ellen (Nell) Isabel Quinn that brought my mother Mary Catherine into this world. And my mother Mary's decision to marry Charles Wesley Doyle that brought me and my seven younger siblings into the world. And now twenty-three of my own dear nieces and nephews are having their own children who in turn are making an impact on the world. As I approach the inevitable end of my life in this world, I am already anticipating a time for letting them all go.

EPILOGUE

But in the meantime, I savor each day, each new life, each new friend, including you.

I am grateful that the paths of our lives have intersected in some mysterious way with yours, dear One. And I pray that these stories, words and loves have inspired and encouraged your own stories, words, loves....

Goodbye, my dear. Godspeed, my dear. Be of good heart, my dear, "as we wait in joyful hope...."

Affectionately,

Ellen

P.S. Write a story, a letter, a song about a last thing, a last person in your life. Hold it against your bones. Share it with someone you love. With a community you belong to. Or perhaps with the world!

Acknowledgments

Three communities brought *Dear Uncle Stanley* into being. The Ursulines of Brown County, especially those in the novitiate with me, claimed him as their own uncle beginning with letter number 2 and became correspondents with him as well. They taught me early on that my uncle's letters were meant for a wider world. The Women Writing for (a) Change community in Cincinnati guided the development of my own voice in dialogue with Uncle Stanley's for today's readers. The intergenerational community at the Catholic Leadership Institute provided the momentum and motivation to finish this book and insights into seekers of all ages who, even if not letter writers themselves, long for intentional relationships that manifest God-with-us.

Special thanks to Agatha Fitzgerald, OSU for the mandala that appears across the seasons of this book and still inspires me to hold the center and stretch possibilities in all my own seasons.

In addition, I want to thank these others who supported the publishing of this book: Ursuline Academy of Cincinnati, Ramona Payne, Peg Morse Conway, Maria Rogers O'Rourke, the late Katherine Meyer, Diane Kruse Planicka, the late Michael Fullum, Matt Manion, Lori Blake Tedjeske, Patty Hogan, Cathy Nagy, dozens of faithful friends and my dear family of siblings, cousins, and especially, the nieces.